Open your heart to true love with

The Tarot Guide to Love and Relationships

You hold in your hands the key
to understanding
the complexities and challenges of
ultimate love—as you journey closer
to sharing
your heart with your one true soul mate . . .

Berkley Books by Nancy Shavick

THE TAROT
THE TAROT READER
TRAVELING THE ROYAL ROAD: MASTERING THE TAROT
THE TAROT GUIDE TO LOVE AND RELATIONSHIPS

The Tarot Guide to Love and Relationships

Nancy Shavick

BERKLEY BOOKS, NEW YORK

THE TAROT GUIDE TO LOVE AND RELATIONSHIPS

A Berkley Book / published by arrangement with
the author

PRINTING HISTORY
Berkley edition / January 1993

ISBN: 0-425-13583-7

A BERKLEY BOOK ® ™ 757,375
Berkley Books are published by The Berkley Publishing Group,
200 Madison Avenue, New York, New York 10016.
The name "BERKLEY" and the "B" logo
are trademarks belonging to Berkley Publishing Corporation.

PRINTED IN THE UNITED STATES OF AMERICA

10 9 8 7 6 5 4 3 2 1

For N

Contents

Introduction   1

PART ONE: *Notes on the Tarot Cards and Love*   3

PART TWO: *What Is the Tarot Deck?*   9
  The Pip Cards   11
    The Court Cards   13
  The Trump Cards   14

PART THREE: *Steps for a Card Reading*   17
  Finding the Significator   19
  Notes on Shuffling   21
  Establishing the Subject of the Reading   22
  Laying the Cards into Spreads   25
  Eight Tarot Spreads That Can Be Used
       to Examine Relationships   28
  The Grand Cross   28
  Four Card Spread   30
  The Past, Present, Future Spread   31
  The Master Spread   33
  Soul Mate Search   34
  As Above, So Below   36
  Three Card Spread   38
  Problem/Solution Spread   38

PART FOUR: *The 78 Tarot Cards and Their Love Interpretations*   41

  The Pips   44
    The Swords   44
    The Disks   52
    The Cups   60
    The Wands   70
  The Trumps   80
    The Fool   80
    The Juggler, Magician or Magus   82
    Juno, the High Priestess or
      Female Pope   83
  The Empress   84
  The Emperor   86
  Jupiter, the Pope, Priest or Hierophant   87
  The Lovers or Love   88
  The Chariot   89
  Justice   90
  The Hermit   91
  The Wheel of Fortune   92
  Strength, Force or Fortitude   93
  The Hanged Man   94
  Death   95
  Temperance   96
  The Devil   97
  The Tower or House of God   98
  The Star   100
  The Moon   101
  The Sun   102
  Judgement   103
  The Universe or World   104

PART FIVE: *Eight Tarot Card Readings on Love*   105

Reading One   107
   Three Card Spread   108
Reading Two   109
   Three Card Spread   109
Reading Three   111
   Problem/Solution Spread   111
Reading Four   113
   The Grand Cross   113
   Four Card Spread   119
Reading Five   122
   The Grand Cross   122
   Four Card Spread   129
Reading Six   132
   The Grand Cross   132
   Four Card Spread   139
Reading Seven   141
   The Grand Cross   142
   Four Card Spread   148
Reading Eight   150
   The Grand Cross   151
   Four Card Spread   158

The Tarot Guide to Love and Relationships

Introduction

The Tarot Guide to Love and Relationships is designed to enable its readers to use Tarot readings to discover what is happening in romantic relationships and to find answers to questions about love by analyzing the thoughts, feelings, people, and events in their lives so that they can make the best decisions regarding any troubling matter. This fourth volume in the Tarot series can help readers expand the boundaries of their emotional limitations to create stronger personalities, partnerships, friendships, and home and work environments. This book emphasizes faith, truth, patience, and an open mind as the pathways to personal happiness and liberation on the challenging journey toward love, wholeness, and contentment. *The Tarot Guide to Love and Relationships* explains how to give Tarot card readings utilizing eight different Tarot spreads, reinterprets the 78 Tarot cards in terms of love, and contains eight actual Tarot readings to demonstrate how the Tarot cards can be used to help solve typical problems that emerge during the course of a relationship.

Part One of *The Tarot Guide to Love and Relationships*, "Notes on the Tarot Cards and Love," explains how the Tarot can assist the card reader in making sense of the often chaotic nature of love and of the role that love plays in daily life.

Part Two of this guide, "What Is the Tarot Deck?" describes the 78 cards of the Tarot deck, and Part Three, "Steps for a Card Reading," offers all the information required to immediately be able to give Tarot card readings. It also provides complete instructions on how to use eight different Tarot card spreads to examine what is happening in your love life. Part Four, "The 78 Tarot Cards and Their Love Interpretations," contains a new definition of each Tarot card in terms of its significance in a reading being done to analyze an important relationship.

Part Five, "Eight Tarot Card Readings on Love," presents actual Tarot readings given to women to help answer questions about their romantic problems. The first three Tarot card readings in this section utilize the Three Card Spread and the Problem/Solution Spread, and the final five readings use the Grand Cross Spread followed by a Four Card Spread.

PART ONE

———— ✦ ————

*Notes on the Tarot Cards
and Love*

PART ONE

Though the Tarot deck is considered one of the great mysteries of the last half millennium, the nature of love between the sexes remains almost as enigmatic on a universal scale. Hundreds of books have been written in an effort to help men and women understand their essential differences, but the ultimate question still remains: Will they ever be able to communicate on the same level, experience mutual, positive, loving relationships, and become more complete human beings?

Today women seem to bear the larger part of the burden of daily existence, and they often wonder why they cannot just get on with their lives without a man and avoid all the problems that usually accompany relationships with members of the opposite sex. Unless a woman has the wisdom to know that men almost always bring chaos into their lives and nearly always fall short of their emotional potential, her involvement with a man will drive her crazy, especially if she tries to analyze the differences too closely. She knows though men are often less mature than women, still the fire of love is the single most important factor that touches every life. History has shown that the power of true love can transform even the most miserable human being into a caring and fruitful member of society.

The truth seems to be that a crucial factor in personal growth is taking the risk to love another person. Meeting this challenge requires hard work if two people are to create a union based on mutual respect and the desire to satisfy each other's needs and individuality in order to grow emotionally. Achieving true intimacy with a man is the challenge of a lifetime. If a woman is lucky enough to find a man who is worthy of her time, attention, and affection, she still must recognize that he may never be as open, loving, and communicative as she is, unless she has found that rarest of creatures: a man who is ready and willing to explore the gentle side of his personality.

It is painful and difficult for any woman to live without a man to share her existence, but the unearthly sorrow of being stuck in a relationship with the wrong man is even worse. Perhaps the hardest test of all is to maintain the almost spiritual belief that for each woman there is one man on the planet somewhere—her soul mate—who will recognize and claim her as his own, so that she will have the chance to become a complete woman who is loved unconditionally. She knows if she stays true to herself and develops her strengths and builds up her self-esteem independently of any man, she will ultimately arrive at a time and place where she will meet a compatible partner with whom she can share a monogamous bond based on mutual trust, a bond that will last through the typical crises and struggles that everyone encounters on a daily basis. Though the soul mate union always grows stronger over the years, it is not immune to the hard work and challenges that confront every partnership on earth. In truth, no matter what the tests and difficulties are for a couple, if true love exists between two people and if they are meant to be together in this lifetime, there is not a person or thing in this universe that can ultimately keep them apart.

While cynics of love say there could not possibly be special people roaming the planet looking for their soul mate whose image they carry in their hearts, evolving people know otherwise, and to them the likelihood of meeting their intended partner is a reality of which they are certain. They know the lovers in their romantic history are just a series of archetypes who form a direct pathway to their ultimate archetype, or soul mate. All past experiences simply prepare them for the explosive meeting with their rightful lifetime partner whom they recognize immediately upon arrival. And unlike the relationship with the soul mate, previous "cell mate" relationships are seen as emotional lessons and karmic relationships that never survive; but the union with one's soul mate is truly eternal.

Tarot card readings are the perfect medium to help you get through desperate times. The cards will help you find answers to problems you encounter with the minor male archetypes on the road to finding true love. Readings can replace your anxiety with hard facts that tell you why you are with a certain man and what emotional experiences you need to share with him so you can move on to a higher level and meet your lifetime partner. When you are totally confused about your love life and know the man you are currently involved with is not the ultimate one, Tarot readings can fill the black hole of conflict between you as you struggle to understand your individual intimacy problems. The Tarot helps you get through the lean years of love so you can continue to prepare yourself for your eventual relationship with your one and only soul mate. Tarot readings can assist you in keeping an eye out for karmic entanglements so you do not confuse those who are catalysts to your romantic education with your true soul mate. You can see more clearly through the readings how those who pass through your life are textbook cases for you to study in your ever-evolving education as a loving soul.

PART TWO

———— ✦ ————

What Is the Tarot Deck?

THE PIP CARDS

The Tarot deck consists of 78 cards; 56 of these cards are called the pip cards, or the minor arcana.

The pips are divided into four suits similar to a modern playing card deck. Instead of clubs, spades, hearts, and diamonds as suits, the Tarot has wands, disks, cups, and swords. The four suits of the Tarot deck correspond to the four elements and four types of activity:

THE SUITS AND THEIR MEANINGS

SUIT	ELEMENT	ACTIVITIES
wand	fire	creativity, energy, action, passion, and spirit
disk	earth	actualization, construction, money, talents, and material things
cup	water	receptivity, soulfulness, emotions, intuition, love, imagination, and visualization

| sword | air | realization, the mind and intellect, communication, thought processes, and decisions |

In each suit there are ten numbered cards (ace through ten) and four court cards (King, Queen, Knight, and Page). The ace is the earliest, most primordial form of the element, and the ten of each suit is the maximum manifestation of the quality of the element. The two through nine are valuable lessons that nurture a slow evolution or ripening as the individual gains control over and consciousness of the activities of the element.

WANDS build toward constructive passionate energy.
DISKS build toward physical security.
CUPS build through emotional fulfillment.
SWORDS build through increased wisdom and knowledge.

NUMERICAL SIGNIFICANCE OF THE PIP CARDS

NUMBER	MEANING
ace	unity of force available within the element; seeds that pave the way for the fullness of the ten; the arrival of something new and powerful

NUMBER	MEANING
two	simple, pure, easy, and early combinations of the element
three	strong creation through the element, leading to advancement and growth
four	stability and structure achieved through the element
five	unusual demands, challenges, and difficulties with the element
six	great usability through a connection of all forces in the suit
seven	individual application of the suit; an adaptation of the element to your own style
eight	seriousness and intensity of the suit leaning toward permanency
nine	substantial and long-lasting expansion of the element
ten	maximum, firm, and fully developed manifestation of the suit

The Court Cards

Within each suit there are four court cards: King, Queen, Knight, and Page.

KINGS are commanding male figures, mature rulers.

QUEENS are commanding female figures, mature rulers.

KNIGHTS are active male figures, more servile than Kings.

PAGES are youthful and devoted apprentices or messengers of their element.

A King and a Knight will not necessarily symbolize a male, nor will a Queen always indicate a female. The personality descriptions of the court cards represent dispositions and temperaments regardless of gender. An abundance of court cards indicates the involvement of many people with the subject of the reading. Court cards can also represent changing facets of one's own destiny.

THE TRUMP CARDS

The remaining 22 cards of the Tarot deck are called the trump cards, or the major arcana. The trumps have their own numerical hierarchy and are numbered 0 to 21 (or 1 to 22), beginning with the Fool and ending with the Universe. Both the names of the trumps and their order can vary from deck to deck.

NUMBER	TITLE OF THE TRUMP CARD
0	The Fool
1	The Juggler, Magician, or Magus
2	Juno, the High Priestess or Female Pope
3	The Empress
4	The Emperor
5	Jupiter, the Pope, Priest, or Hierophant
6	The Lovers or Love
7	The Chariot
8	Justice
9	The Hermit
10	The Wheel of Fortune
11	Strength, Force, or Fortitude
12	The Hanged Man
13	Death
14	Temperance
15	The Devil
16	The Tower or House of God
17	The Star
18	The Moon
19	The Sun
20	Judgement
21	The Universe or World

The trump cards are more enigmatic and visually complex than the pip cards. It is believed that the symbols and figures with which they are decorated project a wide range of cultural and mythological associations. The clothing that adorns the figures, the objects surrounding them, and their postures and gestures are all considered important to their interpretation.

The major arcana carry spiritual force wherever they appear in a Tarot reading. The events they represent are destined; they are inevitable lessons that guide a thinking, feeling soul toward maturation.

PART THREE

———— ✦ ————

Steps for a Card Reading

A Tarot reading takes place when a reader interprets her own cards or translates a reading for another person who is known as the inquirer. The reading consists of shuffling the cards and laying them out into systematic patterns called spreads. Spreads create the scenario of the reading and place the cards in a time sequence. The meanings of the cards are interpreted in conjunction with their placement in the spread in an effort to answer the inquiry brought to the reading.

FINDING THE SIGNIFICATOR

Before you begin to read the Tarot cards you must find the significator. This card represents the inquirer while establishing the subject of the reading.

To determine the significator, one of the eight King or Queen court cards is chosen to symbolize the inquirer. This is done astrologically. Ask the inquirer what his or her zodiac sign is; if the inquirer does not know this information, use this table to discover it:

BIRTH DATE	ZODIAC SIGN
March 21–April 19	Aries
April 20–May 20	Taurus
May 21–June 21	Gemini
June 22–July 22	Cancer
July 23–August 22	Leo
August 23–September 22	Virgo
September 23–October 23	Libra
October 24–November 21	Scorpio
November 22–December 21	Sagittarius
December 22–January 19	Capricorn
January 20–February 18	Aquarius
February 19–March 20	Pisces

When you have determined the sign of the inquirer, use the following table to identify his or her significator. If you are reading your own cards, apply this same method to ascertain your significator. For those born on the cusps of signs (very early or very late in a sign), choose the sign that you feel most in tune with.

ZODIAC SIGN	FEMALE	MALE
Aries, Leo, Sagittarius	Queen of wands	King of wands
Taurus, Virgo, Capricorn	Queen of disks	King of disks
Gemini, Libra, Aquarius	Queen of swords	King of swords
Cancer, Scorpio, Pisces	Queen of cups	King of cups

Therefore, if the inquirer is a man born on June sixth, he is a Gemini, and his significator is the King of swords. If the inquirer is a woman born on January fourth, she is a Capricorn, so her significator is the Queen of disks.

NOTES ON SHUFFLING

You begin the card reading by shuffling the Tarot deck before you lay the cards out into Tarot spreads. The instructions are the same whether a card reader is interpreting her own cards or reading for an inquirer. The only difference is that the inquirer shuffles the deck *after* the reader shuffles and *before* the cards are laid out into the Tarot spreads. The last person to shuffle the cards before they are laid down is *always* the person whose cards are being read. The shuffling process is *always* used between spreads in a reading.

Try to keep the cards facing the same direction when you shuffle the deck. If the cards become a mixture of right side up and upside down, simply put them right side up as you turn them over into a spread. The cards are always laid out facing the reader. The inquirer should sit directly across from the reader, even though the cards will appear upside down from her vantage point.

ESTABLISHING THE SUBJECT OF THE READING

After the significator has been identified, the reading begins. If you are reading for yourself, take the deck in your hands and concentrate on the matter you want information about as you ask the cards for clarity and guidance.

Shuffle the deck three times. If you are reading for an inquirer, ask him or her to shuffle the deck three times after you do. Once the cards are shuffled, separate the deck into the four subject piles:

  Work and Business
  Love and Partnership
  Trouble and Conflict
  Money and Material Matters

The reader lays the deck face down and cuts it twice from right to left:

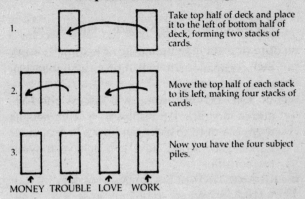

1. Take top half of deck and place it to the left of bottom half of deck, forming two stacks of cards.

2. Move the top half of each stack to its left, making four stacks of cards.

3. Now you have the four subject piles.

↑   ↑   ↑   ↑
MONEY TROUBLE LOVE WORK

Once you have divided the deck into four piles, pick up each pile, turn it over, and sort through it until you find the significator in one of the stacks. In the case of the Gemini man, you would search through each pile, from right to left, until you find the King of swords.

If you find the significator (in our example, the King of swords) in the Work pile, this will become the first subject-combination of the reading. Now put all of the cards together again and shuffle them. Ask the inquirer to shuffle them, too. Then break them up once more into the four subject piles. If during your second subject search you find the King of swords in the Money pile, the subject-combination will be a blend of these two areas, Work and Money.

These subjects are topics, or categories, that represent a combination of problems, activities, and concerns that the spread will illustrate and further define.

The Meanings of the Subject-Combinations

WORK AND WORK: emphasis of reading is work and occupation; it will discuss activities you must undertake.

WORK AND LOVE: reading will discuss effort required in your relationships with other people; there is a need to ascertain how a love alliance affects your work; how you behave in your relationships.

WORK AND TROUBLE: changes necessary in your workplace, where problems arise over your output or involvement; difficulties you have working with others; cause of disharmony and possible solutions; need to analyze and adjust how you apply your creative energy.

WORK AND MONEY: making substantial gains in your work; receiving money or other rewards for your dedication to a project; realizing how you can develop your talents; how you deal with things on a practical level; constructive action.

LOVE AND LOVE: unions emphasized; reading will be a complete discussion of a love relationship or partnership.

LOVE AND TROUBLE: crises, problems, and adjustments in love relationships and partnerships; disharmony in unions and alliances.

LOVE AND MONEY: symbolizes a need for a deeply devoted union or a firm partnership; indicates that a relationship is finally materializing.

TROUBLE AND TROUBLE: problems caused by your personality; disturbances in interpersonal relationships; major changes under way, which reading will illustrate.

TROUBLE AND MONEY: problems with utilization of talents; money difficulties.

MONEY AND MONEY: emphasis of reading is accomplishment, making things happen and actualizing desires; reading will discuss your current material circumstances.

Once you have ascertained the subject-combination, the reading moves on to the spreads.

LAYING THE CARDS INTO SPREADS

There are many Tarot spreads to choose from depending on what you want to discover through a reading. In this section of *The Tarot Guide to Love and Relationships*, you will find eight spreads: the Grand Cross; the Four Card Spread; the Past, Present, Future Spread; the Master Spread; Soul Mate Search; As Above, So Below; Three Card Spread; and Problem/Solution Spread. The instructions for laying the cards into the spreads, the meanings of the placements, and the interpretation of each arrangement are included in the "Eight Tarot Spreads" section, which follows.

To interpret the spread, you must read carefully through the explanation of that spread and look up the meaning of each card in Part Four of this guide, "The 78 Tarot Cards and Their Love Interpretations." Find the descriptions of the card that apply to the relationship problems you are examining through your card reading. Then fit the card into the position in the spread where the card surfaces. The spread placement where the card lands defines how you apply the meaning of the card in the scenario being created by the spread.

Read the spread as though the cards are the details of a story held together in a plot represented by the Tarot spread. Look at the cards as forces within a reading that are separate in meaning but form a message collectively. Readings are impressionistic in nature, and learning how to blend the components takes practice and requires intuition and imagination. Random images and associations that pop into your mind are *always* important. You should acknowledge them and tell the inquirer about them. Continually pay attention to cards that appeared earlier in the spread and tie their meaning into the developing scenario. As you analyze the spread, look at the spread placement and blend it together with the definition of the card that most applies to the matter being examined through the reading.

As you now know, the first step in a Tarot reading is to take the deck into your hands and shuffle it three times. If you are reading for an inquirer, have her shuffle the Tarot deck after you shuffle it. Then lay the cards down in the spread positions according to the order in which they appear, drawing one card after another off the top of the deck. When you have interpreted a spread to your satisfaction, gather all the cards and bring the deck back together. Try to keep the cards facing in the same direction. When you read for another person, the cards usually get mixed up, but you can turn them right side up as you turn the cards over to interpret the spread. *Remember*, if you are reading for an inquirer, you (the reader) must collect the cards between spreads and shuffle the deck three times before handing the deck over to the inquirer. The cards are placed into a spread *after* the inquirer has shuffled. The reader should ask the inquirer to concentrate on her question as she shuffles the deck. The cards that appear in the spread respond to the questions posed to the deck during the shuffling process. When you sit down to read, ask the Tarot deck specific questions and focus on receiving wisdom and guidance during the shuffling process so your interpretation will be crystal clear. Do not be intimidated by the enigmatic pictures on the faces of the cards as you turn them over in the spread. Remember, all you have to do is look up the meanings of the cards in this guide, which is user-friendly and not meant to be confusing or elusive; it is designed to facilitate discovery and increase your awareness.

The Tarot is articulate to the point of eloquence once you know what the cards mean and how to utilize the deck in a reading. When you properly connect the cards' visual attributes to their meaning and can translate what they symbolize in the people, events, and circumstances of your love life, you can give Tarot readings that can change the course of your destiny or bring to light the psychological and spiritual truths behind the drama of your existence. Do not be fatalistic with a reading; look forward to the prospect of using the cards as a tool for finding out what is really going on behind the spectacle of reality. You will grow to love the Tarot as you receive uncanny, nearly miraculous readings that accurately describe what is happening in your love life and what will come to pass in your future relationships with men.

EIGHT TAROT SPREADS THAT CAN BE USED TO EXAMINE RELATIONSHIPS

The Grand Cross

The most classic and well-known spread is the Grand Cross or Celtic Cross. The layout for the Grand Cross consists of eleven cards.

THE GRAND CROSS

1. Self Card

2. Present Environment

3. Obstacle

4. Hope and Dream

5. Difficulty in the Past

6. Last of the Present

7. First of the Future

8. Future Environment

9. Outer Influence

10. Hope and Fear

11. Outcome

The Meanings of the Eleven Positions in the Grand Cross

1. Self Card: The self card symbolizes the inquirer at the time of the reading and describes her current state of mind or her position in the matter.

2. Present Environment: This card represents the atmosphere at the time of the reading; the current environment as it influences the self card.

3. Obstacle: Any card in this position is an immediate obstacle in your path, and you must acknowledge its influence on the course of the reading. It is important to accept the influence of this card even if you ultimately decide to ignore, fight, or enjoy what it symbolizes. The obstacle can be a block in your way of thinking or an activity you must undertake reluctantly in order to meet the outcome of a reading.

4. Hope and Dream: This card indicates what you want more than anything and what you should be striving for, or it can represent wishes fulfilled in their purest form without any compromise. This position is separate from the rest of the spread. It carries the force of a delicate romantic dream that you maintain regardless of what is happening in reality.

5. Difficulty in the Past: You have to meet the challenge of the card that falls in this position. A past event has been causing trouble and making things hard for you even though you have grown through the difficulties. This position indicates that the past event symbolized by this

card will no longer be a hindrance but will give you support in the future.

6. Last of the Present: The card in this position stands for whatever has happened just prior to the reading.

7. First of the Future: This card represents what will occur immediately after the reading.

8. Future Environment: The card that falls in this spot represents the atmosphere of the future.

9. Outer Influence: The ninth card stands for the effect that other people have on the outcome of the reading and how they will influence the relationship. The card indicates the behavior you can expect from family, friends, and acquaintances.

10. Hope and Fear: This position carries a sharp, decisive warning and is the turning point of the reading. You should work to attain what this card represents if you wish to meet the outcome of the reading. It is the resolve that you fear most, although it would successfully conclude the matter that so concerns you. This is the moment of truth, the ultimate decision you would rather put off indefinitely.

11. Outcome: The card in this position represents the end result of the scenario of the reading. It sums up the entire situation. It also is the lead card for your next reading on the same subject.

Four Card Spread

For the Four Card Spread, you lay the top four cards out from left to right. The meaning of the

how the love partners are dealing with their current romantic issues at the time of the reading (the present) and what changes will occur at a future date on all three levels established by this spread (material, love, and liberation).

The Master Spread

THE MASTER SPREAD

1	2	3	4	5	6	7

1 to 7: EVENTS LEADING UP TO THE PRESENT SITUATION

8	9	10	11	12	13

8 to 13: DESCRIPTION OF THE PRESENT SITUATION

14	15	16	17	18

14 to 18: WHAT OTHER PEOPLE ARE DOING FOR OR AGAINST YOU; THEIR INVOLVEMENT IN THE MATTER

19	20	21	22

19 to 22: THE BEST POSSIBLE FORTUNE YOU CAN ATTAIN IN THE MATTER

23	24

23 and 24: IMMEDIATE SURPRISES CONCERNING THE MATTER

25	26	27	28	29	30	31

25 to 31: FUTURE EVENTS LEADING TO THE OUTCOME

32

32: THE OUTCOME OF THE MATTER

You will use 32 cards in this spread. First, lay them out face down from left to right. Then turn them over and read them in numerical order, line by line. This spread will discuss and illuminate the widest range of variables that are affecting a love relationship. As in the Past, Present, Future Spread, you must learn how to interpret the meaning of a group of cards that fall next to each other. This spread may be too complex to read for another person at first; use it as a quiet internal meditative tool when you want a great deal of information on what is happening with a man you love.

Soul Mate Search

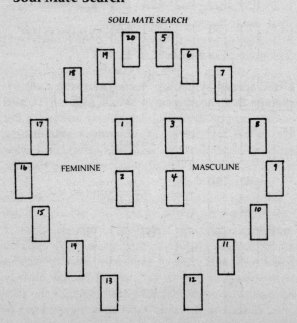

SOUL MATE SEARCH

FEMININE   MASCULINE

This layout examines the stages of development in your relationships with those of the opposite sex in terms of karma brought forth from your childhood experience (cards 1, 2, 3, and 4) with your parents, guardians, or figures of love and authority and how this has influenced your subconscious self-image. Implied in this spread (cards 5 through 20) is the pathway to the ideal person, or soul mate, with whom you could share a mature commitment without repeating as an adult the identical union that your parents may have had and move on to create a union that reflects the highest aspirations for your deeply loving self.

To interpret this spread, begin with cards 1 and 2, which indicate your self-image as a female. The Tarot cards that fall in these two positions show the way you see yourself due to karma taken on from the maternal energy in your life.

For a woman, cards 3 and 4 on the masculine side of the spread symbolize her animus, the male archetype that she attracts to herself naturally, based on her experience with the paternal energy in her life, which has played a large role in establishing the level of her self-esteem. Cards 1 through 4 show the karma taken on by a female through her parents, for better or for worse.

For a man, cards 3 and 4 on the masculine side indicate his self-image as a man due to karma taken on from the fatherly influence in his life. Cards 1 and 2 describe his anima, the female archetype that he unconsciously seeks, based on his experiences with female energy in his past. If he has already released any negativity inherited through the parents, cards 1 to 4 would take on a higher level of meaning and would be indicative of his search for the most pure and complementary soul mate and would show him animating cards 3 and 4 in the most spiritual manner. This man would find his true consort through the activities of the cards that surface in positions 1 and 2. This would of course apply in reverse for a woman reading her cards.

For a female, cards 5 through 12 symbolize what her man has to accomplish psychologically, emotionally, spiritually, and materially on his path to meeting her and through the earliest stages of their relationship, with card 12 defining the nature of the union in its ultimate conclusion. Cards 13 through 20 show what she has to go through in her romantic experience until she is secure in her connection to the right man (card 20).

For a man, cards 13 through 20 depict what his soul mate is going through to find him and at what level her male archetype is currently functioning. Cards 5 through 12 show how he is proceeding on his path to his one true love.

As Above, So Below

This directional spread examines the forces that surround you in your relationship with a man and are therefore influencing your movement and position in life as regards a particular union.

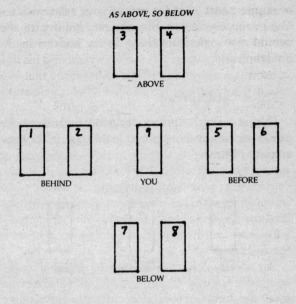

To use this spread, lay the top nine cards out in the arrangement illustrated above. Cards 1 and 2 symbolize your past experiences in love, who or what is behind you that has lost its power over you and no longer influences your life. Cards 3 and 4 describe what crowns you (is above you), environmental factors affecting you, and how you merge with society in general. Cards 5 and 6 have to do with what is before you in your future, what is ahead of you, the outcome of the subject matter of the reading, and who or what is growing more dominant along the horizon of life yet to come. Cards 7 and 8 show what is below or beneath you, what you already have under control, whom you can be certain of as a partner in love, and the forces of support that exist for you in your relationships. Card 9 represents you, the inquirer, and depicts the central core experience that you are undergoing in a relationship.

Three Card Spread

This is a quick spread designed to answer the most specific questions posed to the deck in the least amount of time.

THREE CARD SPREAD

1	2	3
CONDITIONS BROUGHT OVER FROM THE PAST	PRESENT CONDITIONS	WHAT WILL HAPPEN IN THE FUTURE

Read this spread from left to right, interpreting Card 1 as conditions brought over from past romantic experiences as they affect the issue brought to the reading, Card 2 as present relationship conditions, and Card 3 as the outcome of the matter or the direction your involvement will take depending upon the nature of the Tarot card that surfaces there.

Problem/Solution Spread

This layout helps you get to the heart of the reasons why certain difficult romantic experiences happen for a purpose in your life. It analyzes how you can first identify the nature of the problem and constructively deal with it through positive action to resolve old issues that you have chosen to deal with at this time in your life.

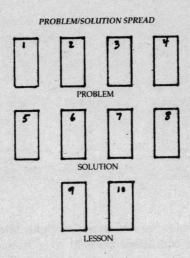

PROBLEM/SOLUTION SPREAD

Lay out ten cards in the above arrangement. Cards 1 through 4 symbolize the current status of the issue and focus on the problem you are currently facing. Cards 5 through 8 show you what course of action will lead to a satisfying solution to the situation. Cards 9 and 10 depict the karmic lessons inherent in this obstacle that you must become aware of so you can change the course of your life pathway for the better.

PART FOUR

— ✦ —

*The 78 Tarot Cards and
Their Love Interpretations*

This section contains numerous descriptions to help the card reader interpret each of the 78 Tarot cards in readings about love and relationships. The descriptions in this guide are more specific than those found in *The Tarot* and *The Tarot Reader* in that they are less abstract in nature and are designed to set off multiple triggers in the mind of the reader.

To utilize these new card definitions, simply read through the Tarot spread placement by placement in numerical order. Look up the meaning of each card in this section of *The Tarot Guide to Love and Relationships*. Find the descriptions of the card that apply to the matter that the Tarot spread is examining; then fit each description into the position of the spread where it surfaces. Where the card lands in the spread placement defines how you apply the meaning of the card in the scenario being created by the spread. Sometimes only one of the descriptions of a Tarot card will make sense to you in terms of what is happening in your love life; often more than one of the definitions will fit into what you are experiencing in reality.

THE PIPS

The Swords

Ace of Swords: Deciding once and for all to see the relationship through to the end; being totally directed toward one man; having a determined attitude toward a man; doing whatever you must to make a relationship work out; struggling to stay optimistic and clearheaded; being true to your word with him; coming through on all promises you make in love; feeling confident that you think exactly the same way about each other.

Two of Swords: Both people are wondering whether the relationship can go any further; relying on an inner trust of each other; believing what he says to the core of your being; having to hold out for a while until you are able to see if he is what you think; knowing there is a higher reason for your being together; thinking about each other constantly; having complete faith in an absolute future together; knowing you should never doubt him as it undermines his confidence; learning to trust him so you can forge a union of easy, fluid communication.

Three of Swords: Feeling that your life is sad because you have no one to love at the time of the reading; knowing that you always get the short end of the stick in love and that this is unfair; the pain of separation; the sadness of missing someone; your heart is breaking; walking around in tears; wondering when your weeping will end; sorrow over the way things used to be; having to move away from or break up with someone you dearly love; showing emotional weakness when you are hurt enough by his behavior to cry; taking the relationship too hard; physically hurting when you are in disharmony with him.

Four of Swords: Trying to decide what to do about a relationship; needing quiet time to think and sort your feelings out; solitude as the only solution to your confusion over him; after much deliberation, coming up with a new way of looking at your situation with him; being apart at first in a relationship because you both need time to reflect and comprehend the value of what is happening between you; he needs space mentally for his line of work; one of you is not talking; the more time he has alone, the better off he will be.

Five of Swords: Having to listen to a lot of grief coming from him or others; having your mental space invaded by his problems or indecision; needing to talk things out together; really listening to what

he says; learning how to handle conflict constructively; bad communication habits between a couple; what
other people think and say about the
relationship and whether you will let
their ideas influence your way of
thinking or not; having to lay down
the law with him; having selfish arguments that are wrecking the peace
of your friendship; not seeing eye to
eye on issues that surround the rela-
tion ship; him not listening or re-
sponding verbally to what you say;
hearing him out even if you do not
agree with him; letting people gossip
about your love life because you do
not care about their speculations; feeling that you have nobody to talk to in
the midst of social insanity.

**Six
of Swords:**   Clear lines of communication being established between you; sensing or discovering that he will come through;
that you will come to understand the
wisdom behind the problems you
have worked out together; that the
pathway to your soul mate is opening
up and becoming obvious; that you
will meet a man easily and soon and
that he will literally be placed in your
path when the time is ripe for such an
encounter; that everything will begin
to go smoothly with a relationship;
traveling into uncharted waters of in-

timacy with a man; meeting of the
minds with a man; your past romantic
experiences suddenly making sense to
you, and seeing quite clearly that there
is a pattern that forms the basis for
your education in the ways of love.

**Seven
of Swords:** To be free to be yourself and do your
own thing; mental liberation from
preconceived notions about love;
thinking and doing for yourself;
establishing your own identity apart
from the relationship; going your
own way if only for a short period of
time; focusing on your life, not his;
confronting the issue of freedom in a
relationship; erasing the scripts of society and other false collective pressures that limit the development of a
friendship; that your union exists in its
own orbit; accepting and allowing privacy, dignity, and individuality to
exist in a relationship; balancing independence so you can easily be alone
as well as together.

**Eight
of Swords:** Feeling blocked in your mind and unable to think clearly about him; that
there are walls of noncommunication
between you that must come down or
the relationship will end; not having a
clue about what to do because you are
totally confused; being liberated from
a union with another that placed you
in a mental prison of sorts and finally

taking part in life again; that everything is on hold in a relationship for the time being; seeing your way through obstacles together; feeling as if you are waking up from a coma after resolving your love problems.

Nine of Swords: Having extreme brain strain due to difficulties with a particular man; mental agony driving you nearly mad; nagging issues about love keeping you up at night; intellectual cruelty and general unkindness being created by you or directed at you by him; anxiety over whether he loves you or not; feeling that you are all alone in the world and that nobody cares for you; having no secrets from each other and how hard that can be sometimes; that the truth of your psychological pain must be exposed to him, and you know it and fear it; he knows if he rejects your love he is doomed to a lifetime of emptiness or worse; that you are starving for understanding from him.

Ten of Swords: Having great difficulty putting up with his depression; not wanting to take on his problems anymore; total exhaustion from the constant strain of a complicated love affair; not wanting to take a relationship another step further; the agony the relationship has put you through has reached a point of maximum overload; his totally non-

supportive attitude is wrecking your
sense of well-being; that the relationship has real problems that will not go
away overnight; that your physical
health has been destroyed by your
problems in love; that through your difficulties with a man you have gained
an extraordinary wisdom about how
relationships work; having a mental
breakdown as the result of an exhaust-
ing romance; you cannot take any
more suffering and you tell him so.

**Page
of Swords:**
That you must listen and watch and
spy to figure out what is going on in a
relationship; a message coming to you
from a man that changes the entire direction of a romance; finally getting specific information from him or about
him that enlightens you to the absolute truth; he will telephone you and
ask you out; he will have somebody
else make a move on his behalf so you
do know he is interested in you; that
he is observing your behavior unbe-
knownst to you before deciding
whether he wants to get involved with
you; that his arrogance is a direct result of his underlying insecurities; that
meeting a new man is like a call to attention you have been waiting for; that
in an established romance you need to
make alternate plans just in case
things do not work out; what you said

to him got through to him in more
ways than one; he will ask you to
marry him.

**Queen
of Swords:**

You are a sharp woman who pushes
for what you want and will not take
no for an answer; in the relationship,
you will have to constantly fight for
yourself; that you are the brains behind a partnership; that you are
smarter than he, and this worries him;
that in a relationship you are the ag-
gressor; that you have really brilliant
ideas about what you and he should
do together; that you must constantly
push him to grow; that you speak your
mind often and harshly; that you may
need to withhold sex or warmth from
him in order for your plans to work;
that at a certain point you must dictate
what will happen next; that you are
always analyzing and plotting and can
never relax and just let a romance unfold naturally; speaking up for yourself in an argument with your mate.

**Knight
of Swords:**

He is moving as fast as he can; he is a
man who does not have time for love;
that he's a busy man who has too
many things to do and is never there
when you need him; that because of
his work he is constantly traveling;
someone brilliant and quick-witted
who is interested in you; an intelligent
person who inspires you to get your

work done quickly and with great diligence; a man who leaves a trail of broken hearts behind him; a man who is
not easily affectionate or does not like
to be touched; an emotionally insecure
man who avoids intimacy because he
fears appearing vulnerable or getting
hurt; someone who is interested in you
but is reluctant to show his feelings;
a man who pursues you but panics
and flees once you begin to warm up
to him.

**King
of Swords:**
A man who is probably a miserable
human being; a man who acts like a
cold fish sexually; a man who says he
does not need you in his life, whether
that is true or not; a man who feels that
he is beyond desiring a woman and
that relationships are troublesome and
a waste of time; a man who is controlling, demanding, and difficult to
please; a person who is used to getting
his own way; someone who is completely selfish; one who feels that his
role is to exert power and authority
over women; a man who has no fun in
life because he is too serious; a partner
who may be angry, destructive, and
even sadistic in his behavior toward
you; a man you want to support you
one hundred percent; a man who may
want to live without a companion; a
man who has trouble fitting a relation-

ship in with his work; a man who
comes through for a woman once he
makes the decision to do so himself.

The Disks

**Ace
of Disks:**
Meeting someone new to whom you
are immediately attracted; a friendship
that has the potential to grow into a union that is grounded in reality; that you
are trying to plant seeds for the future
in a current romance; that a man is trying to impregnate you; learning to live
in the moment with him and not in the
past or future; that you have not yet
seen how capable or talented he really
is; the early stages of a relationship before practical matters intercede; having
a one-dimensional view of a man because you hardly know him yet; someone you admire comes to visit you at
home, unannounced; preparing for a
relationship long before the right partner appears; working hard on building
a strong foundation in an already existing union.

**Two
of Disks:**
Feeling uncertain about a man; both of
you having trouble making specific
plans together; a choice needs to be
made either by you or by him; a
friendship that is in limbo and does
not seem to be growing or ending;

traveling with him; changing residences so as to be together; avoiding merging financially with another; not getting into a deep commitment with a man; the times when you want to tell him to get lost; the fact that every long-term relationship experiences hills of happiness and valleys of doubt and despair; leaving a partner behind for practical reasons; not having enough money to do all the things you want to do together; having trouble choosing between two basically great men.

Three of Disks: Knowing that the relationship will work out no matter what; sticking with a guy as you struggle to grow closer to each other; much effort needs to go into a partnership that requires a much stronger foundation so it can stand up to the test of time; some level of commitment has been reached in a union you want to be permanent; either he or you are out of a job and actively seeking employment; ending a relationship in a friendly manner, and both people realize how much they have grown together; that a relationship has reached the end of a cycle of development and must move on to meet greater challenges on a practical level.

Four of Disks: You need to get your finances in order; buying possessions for him; purchasing useful items together; him making you feel totally secure about the relationship; that you will meet a man who will spend money on you or set you up financially; feeling that you deserve to have everything you want; feeling certain of the fact that he is behind you one hundred percent no matter what condition you are in or what bad luck you are having; you want to know how much he is worth monetarily; material resources are an issue in your relationship; a person who approaches you with a job offer is really interested in you romantically; supporting you financially is his method of reserving you for himself; being too possessive of a man and suffocating him by holding on too tight.

Five of Disks: Money problems coming between you and your man; sharing a simple lifestyle with your mate; having the same material values; between the two of you there is a definite meeting of the minds; being secretive about money for a reason; someone is hiding wealth or poverty; two lost souls finding each other in the world and feeling grateful for their bond; a romantic breakup that makes you feel orphaned or abandoned; feeling that one of you is a financial or professional failure; getting through tough times together; that you will carry on together without any

major material changes; you know
you have no choice but to remain a
couple; he feels like a bum about how
he is behaving or how he runs his life;
hanging out with a man because you
are needy or homeless.

**Six
of Disks:**

Figuring out how to share your lives;
having a mutually balanced exchange
of material resources with another;
that you only want what is fair from
him; that both of you need to take care
of yourselves financially even if you
merge your lives in a practical sense;
being unconditionally accepted for
who you are by a man; learning how
to give of yourself and always be there
for someone; assisting your partner
with his work because you want him
to succeed; seeking out people who
can help your man get ahead in his career; someone who is philanthropic or
a benefactor to you suddenly becomes
interested in you romantically; that
your partner possesses skills you do
not have and vice versa, which makes
you complementary on a practical
level.

**Seven
of Disks:**

Having to wait a long time before you
can see someone again; letting a relationship develop slowly under the
best possible conditions; meeting a
great guy but knowing it may take
months before you will be able to start

a friendship with him; a man and woman who give each other time to get ready for a relationship because both have to grow into it; being too immature to get together with a man yet.

Eight of Disks: A relationship that will require a great deal of effort to begin and maintain; working on the same issues over and over again with a man before you both get it right; someone who is repeating the same problematic behavior day after day; having to expend physical energy for the sake of your partnership whether you shoulder domestic responsibilities or have to work alongside your man in a professional sense; that a person you are involved with is an artisan or just a hard worker who is dedicated to a particular skill or craft; making the same mistakes ad infinitum in love; tough times that ultimately bring a couple closer together; having patience while a man goes to school or takes on an internship or apprenticeship so he can realize his career dreams.

Nine of Disks: Solving the problem of how you two can be together; a man and woman who have it all and appreciate their blessings; that the relationship will work out if both partners apply themselves to forging a rock-solid union; realizing your own self-worth; knowing that your talents and abilities are extremely valuable to your man and knowing that he is aware of this as well; being able to take for granted that he will always be there for you; due to the true love of a good man, you finally feel comfortable with yourself; someone who inspires you to request more money for your work or at your place of employment; meeting a man due to his interest in your work after he seeks you out to tell you how much he admires your creations or concepts; two people who are dedicated to the environment, to animal rights, or to studying the wonders of the natural world; finding a man through your interest in same; a man and woman who share their home, money, or knowledge generously with others.

Ten of Disks: A wealthy man who will set you up financially or who has the connections to make your greatest dreams come true; a man who will offer you the traditional package of marriage, home, and children; deciding whether you will say yes or no to a serious proposal coming from a mature man; sharing financial responsibilities with your partner; two lives merging both socially and materially; feeling that you want to start a family; being lucky enough to have enough resources so

that you and he can set up a life together; desiring only the best for each
other; coming to terms with yourself
as a complete human being; being
aware of cultures and civilizations you
have shared in past lives; an inheri-
tance coming to you or your man; a
person who comes from a rich family
or a distinguished background; a man
who is very close to his family or who
lives with them; a man whom you
have always admired professionally
and now are involved with romantically.

**Page
of Disks:** A younger person or an assistant who
works for you, with whom you de-
velop a romance; a man who does not
feel good enough, rich enough, or
ready enough to be with you; having
to sign legal documents before becoming the official partner of another; a
man playing a supporting role to you
in your career; the object of your romantic interest is also your manager,
secretary, teacher, or student; reading
a book or article or hearing a song a
guy has written and falling in love
with him through his work; a man you
meet on the job; a man who supports
you financially while you go to school
or while you take a job that pays very
little money; a man who is always
there to cheer you up when you are

down; a man and woman who are devoted to each other and who work hard every day to make their union stronger.

Queen of Disks: Your financial independence as a factor in a relationship; having to get your career or material world together; you paying the bills or supporting a man; to be the woman behind the man or the creative resource from which he draws his ideas and strategies; a woman who is only out for money or prestige from a man and is not in love with him; sleeping with a man because he could advance your career; a woman who does charity work for others; a wife and mother who nurtures everyone in her life without hesitation; you handling the family money or budget for the household; being what is termed a good woman; becoming a healer or a caretaker of the earth.

Knight of Disks: A man who means what he says; a man who backs up his romantic intentions with concrete action; someone who lives in the country or loves being surrounded by the natural world; a simple, unpretentious person who is neither colorful nor controversial nor particularly exciting; what you see is what you get with a guy; one who keeps his head down to earth and is an

extremely hard worker; a man who is
always there for you and you know it;
a peaceful person whose gentleness
and love of simple pleasures is a
breath of fresh air in your life; a man
who will impregnate you.

**King
of Disks:**
A partner whose business ideas help
your career to grow; a man who comes
through for you big time; a man who
offers you a secure life both financially
and emotionally; a man providing for
and protecting you; a person whose
main concern is that you are happy
and who will do everything he can to
bring you great joy; a man who buys
you a home or feeds you because he
loves you, not because he has to; a
good man but one who is not overly
passionate or sexual; a quiet or with-
drawn person who is a stable love interest for you; a wealthy man with
whom you become lifetime partners
and gladly share all material burdens;
a guy you meet while traveling for
business or to purchase major possessions; a man who trusts you and has
complete confidence in your abilities.

The Cups

**Ace
of Cups:**
Starting over with renewed caring in
an already established union; being

madly in love; knowing that you may get only one crack at true love; love being at the heart of all you do; pregnancy; a deep and lasting happiness with another; learning to love yourself before you can love another; a man you never tire of being with; just looking at your beloved fills your soul with joy; a man who opens you up sexually; your feelings for him are a constant source of wonder to you; the ecstasy that characterizes the earliest stages of a relationship; taking time for love in the midst of a hectic life; meeting your soul mate for the first time and experiencing an immediate and total physical attraction to him unlike anything you have ever felt before; beginning to heal your emotional self with the help of your partner; meeting someone you were romantically involved with in a past life and feeling an instant bond with him; knowing that he is truly in love with you.

Two of Cups: Following your heart and going wherever love is; true love; an equal exchange of pure emotion between two people; a simple union that is devoid of complications and is therefore lucky for the happy couple; even if you and your partner do not stay together you will always be in love with each other; he requires sympathy from you or vice versa; intimacy that focuses on mutual ecstasy, joy, and satisfaction; being loved by a man as you have never been loved before; knowing that he is as attracted to you as you are to him; two people who have only the best intentions for each other; a relationship in which the feelings are reciprocal; a harmonious friendship between two lovers; forming a creative partnership with the person you love; a spiritual soul mate with whom you share everything except your physical body.

Three of Cups: Enjoying the fruits of life with a man regardless of where the relationship is headed; there is something for you to celebrate about love and being alive; being deliriously happy; meeting someone and just knowing you two would have a really great time together because of an instant compatibility between you; meeting someone at a party or in a casual social atmosphere; his or your excessive partying as an issue in the relationship; keep going out and meeting people and saying yes to dates; being thrilled because you are about to see a man to whom you are deeply attracted; being ready for a sensual and playful affair with a man.

Four of Cups: Having trouble figuring a relationship out; being distant from your own feel-

ings; an offer of love from a man that
you do not want to accept for some
reason; you are unsure about the exact
nature of your affection for a guy; that
one of you is emotionally unavailable
at the time of the reading; that he tells
you he does not know what he wants
from your relationship or how he really feels about you; having to get
stronger emotionally; not wanting to
see someone again; eating your heart
out over a man; having trouble con-
centrating because of love problems;
slow withdrawal from a union gone
bad, even if you continue to live with
the person or stay married to him; being in love with someone you cannot
be with or discuss with anyone; after
a breakup of a union you take time to
analyze what went wrong or why you
behaved the way you did with him.

**Five
of Cups:**

Going backwards in a relationship; a
love affair that does not work out,
though you remain in love with the
man; unfulfilled emotions; accepting
that you can only be friends with
someone you long to be intimate with;
a canceled date; a broken vow; you
thought the relationship was on, but it
is off; he fails to come through as he is
unable to meet you halfway; trying to
handle physical rejection as best you
can; the end of a relationship makes

you feel as though your life is over and you have no idea how you will carry on; knowing in your heart that a man is not your soul mate and that he is just a passing archetype in your love life; an alliance does not work out because, although you love the guy, you know he is not the right person for you; lost love; failed relationships in your past that have made you conscious of how to deal with love gone bad.

Six of Cups: Growing together with someone through love; learning to compromise emotionally; rejuvenating a relationship that has strayed off course; your union with him is not over even if it seems that way at the time of the reading; feeling as much in love with him now as you did when you first fell hard for each other; radiating joy to others due to the inner happiness you feel; rediscovering each other after a period of estrangement; being able to express your feelings openly to someone without fear or hesitation; having a lover in your life after a long dry spell; taking a holiday from reality with your man; enjoying pure sensuality with a positive and joyful man.

Seven of Cups: Having many dreams about all the fantastic things you could do together with a man; a fantasy relationship that exists only in your head, as the other person does not feel the way you do; your mind going wild and crazy over love; having an illicit love affair that nearly drives you mad because you cannot speak of it to anyone; that caring for a man means nothing unless he equally shares your view; having premonitions of your man long before he actually enters your life; utilizing your imagination and powers of creative visualization to draw a suitable partner into your world; dating more than one man and having to narrow down your field and become romantically involved with just one; using your sixth sense to tap into the truth about someone with whom you are in love; receiving information about him through your dreams, which are projections of your fears.

Eight of Cups: Wanting to know what his deepest thoughts are about you; being emotionally strong and completely faithful romantically; making a relationship decision based on serious morals and values; doing what is right with a man; being committed to someone from the depths of your soul; you being capable of the most devoted behavior in a union; sharing dreams or telepathy with a man whom you cannot be with in reality; to always be there for him day and night; someone who is worthy of your dedication.

Nine:
of Cups

Feeling that you care very much about someone and that your love for him will never die; timelessness understood in an established alliance; a lifetime of happiness together; that he will be your partner for eternity; knowing that he will give you joy your whole life through; your love for a man leading you closer to your true self; real emotional maturity; you are secure in the fact that a man adores you and that his love for you will grow stronger over time; being aware that he accepts you no matter what you look like, do, or say; a relationship that makes you a more nurturing person; having a healthy and productive lifestyle that you can enjoy on into the future; you are finally mature enough to appreciate true intimacy.

Ten
of Cups:

Being more in love with him than with any man you have known before; being deliriously happy when you two are together; wanting to start a family with him because you feel he would make the perfect partner and father; having a bond with him that nobody can tear apart; emotional serenity and security; being totally sincere with a man; having it all because you have each other; his love makes you feel like a complete human being; he knows that you fit perfectly into every area of his life and that you accept his personality and habits and would never try to change him; having the best times with him and your children; creating a harmonious social life together; projecting peaceful vibrations as a couple and embracing others in the name of love; meeting a great guy through mutual friends.

Page of Cups: Someone who will not make the first move romantically; a man being really nice; a youthful admirer who is besotted with you; younger people or children as an important influence on your relationship with a man; an immature person who needs to be trained as a lover or a serious boyfriend; someone for whom you may have to wait years in order to see what kind of man he will become; his getting to the point of surrendering the child in himself to you; someone who deserves your sympathy or shows you compassion; a man who is starving for love and affection; a man who is having trouble coming to terms with his feelings because he is afraid of losing control if he falls in love with you; a virginal sort of guy who is inexperienced in romance; a shy person who is afraid of having his heart broken by you; someone who has a negative attitude toward love because of bad luck with women in the past; being emotionally attached to the memory of a person who hurt you.

Queen of Cups: Learning to roll with the punches and the ups and downs in love; being less analytical than you have been previously when it comes to your judgment of men; becoming unfocused and changeable because you are following vague dreams of romance; being needy and clinging to a man; a woman who has to get her life together and become stronger emotionally; offering the cup of love to someone you adore; a man who bounces ideas off of you because he admires your instincts about people and business; willfully drawing a man closer to you; a love affair putting you into a trance and making you feel detached from reality; a woman who chooses to love men who are completely different from her socially or financially; you being unreliable in a relationship or unfaithful to your partner without really knowing why; a woman who radiates warmth to all people regardless of how strange or even dangerous they are; being sympathetic and forgiving to a lover who has betrayed you; letting men use or abuse you emotionally; being the "other woman"; choosing an older man as a lover.

Knight
of Cups:

A man being wishy-washy and changeable about his feelings for you; not being able to believe a word he says; fearing that none of his promises mean a thing in reality; him offering you all sorts of wonderful invitations that he has no intention of coming through on; that he is under the influence of alcohol or drugs, or mentally unstable; that emotionally he is out of control; a man who will invite you to be with him or go to an event as his date but who does not necessarily desire more than a companion; a man who is shallow with women and who has trouble with real intimacy; a person who will hurt you if you fall in love with him; his behavior serves to mask his emotional insecurity; someone who only wants to party with you; a man who makes decisions about a relationship as he goes along and has no real plan and changes his mind constantly; a man who is irresponsible and fickle with women.

King
of Cups:

A man who is closemouthed about his feelings, which he can express only in an explosively dramatic manner; a man who loves you but will not tell you so because he first wants to observe you and test your behavior; one of you is not being honest about your personal finances; being secretive with

your partner; he offers you rewards if
you come back to him after you break
up; a man who is physically far away
from you or unreachable for other reasons; there could be an emotional tug-
of-war going on between you and him;
that a relationship is an obstacle for
you and a distracting quantity in your
life; a wise businessman with a really
good idea that you could develop professionally; someone you have to
negotiate with personally or professionally on a highly sophisticated
level; a man who cares deeply about
you but who does not express his emotions; being involved in a controlling
and destructive relationship with
an inhibited and complicated man;
having an almost telepathic understanding with your partner; meeting
someone overseas or being in love
with a man who is a different nation-
ality than you; a man who deserves
your respect; a man who loves to give
and receive gifts.

The Wands

**Ace
of Wands:**   Making an effort to let him know you
care; leaving the past behind and entering a fresh new phase in a relationship; starting over with a renewed

interest in each other; wanting things
to be different between you; him
wanting a physical union with you
even though you have just met; trying
to create a life that is healthy and positive for both of you; a man who offers
you new and exciting experiences,
which you are thrilled to discover and
learn from; he pushes you to overcome
your fears; that he deeply desires you;
that the two of you need to change
your career focus and begin a new
venture together; a relationship that
challenges you and requires all your
energy; being completely confident in
love; preparing for the future together;
falling in love revitalizes your soul.

**Two
of Wands:**
Taking the initiative in love and seeking him out without fear of rejection;
you having to take on the masculine
role in a relationship; feeling desperate, as though you must have a man
or else; being persistent and not giving
up on a guy or bailing out of his life
because of his problems; if you see romantic potential in someone, you are
willing to be forward and contact him
through the mail or the telephone;
having to go out into the world to find
him or to bring someone back into
your life; pushing him to make a decision; forcing a relationship with him;
willfully trying to trap a man; that both

people need to maneuver their own ships for a while; both partners must determine what their individual desires are and which way they want the friendship to go; becoming energetically involved in his work; that the relationship will receive no assistance from others in order to come together.

Three of Wands: Expressing yourself in a pure, open, and honest way with a man without fear of rejection; making an effort to socialize in his sphere of activity; feeling that you have said all you need to say to him; that you are romantically interested in more than one man; his interest in you inspires your creative work; being comfortable with the current status of your relationship; that you admire him and his work; enjoying a phase of casual dating; total passionate commitment to a man; telling someone you love him for the first time; knowing how you function when you are in love; making amends to those you have hurt romantically in the past; showing your thanks to those who have selflessly supported you previously.

Four of Wands: The peace and quiet of a steady domicile that you share with your partner where you both can increase your creative powers; wanting to have a beautiful and serene atmosphere where you reside; establishing or purchasing a home together where you can be happy and which you can share with others; security and stability as by-products of a passionate union; his caring gives you a closer connection to your true self than you could have achieved on your own; contentment with the arrangement you have forged between you; being pleased with your mutual social life; you know what makes you happy; the feeling of having finally arrived at the right destination romantically; knowing that you have a right to joy and happiness; being a peacemaker who settles the arguments that surround your relationship with each other; being comfortable with your feelings for a man.

Five of Wands: A man caring so much about you that he finds it hard to let you go; both of you are deeply affected by your mutual desire; wild passionate love that will never fade away but will only grow stronger over time; a physical chemistry that gets hotter and hotter; sexual obsession; him feeling as though he must have you no matter what the consequences are; fighting with each other about a particular issue outside of the relationship; one of

you is creating arguments in an effort
to destroy your friendship; a tug-of-
war is going on between you; one of
you is afraid of intimacy, and this is
causing problems in your alliance; a
couple who have to be in discord before they can get physically passionate; you refuse to hear him out or he
does not listen to your complaints; you
both get involved in a social cause,
and this brings you closer together;
taking risks in love; acting as if you
hate someone when you really like
him; feeling suspicious of your own
desires; getting involved in a
spontaneous and fiery love affair.

**Six
of Wands:**   That you two have achieved a creative
victory by staying together through
any rough periods; you have won an
arduous battle over a man, and now
you can relax and enjoy the rewards
of the struggle; discussing your feelings for each other openly and easily;
choosing to be with a man whom others have rejected; nobody else likes the
person you are in love with, and you
must fight for your right to be with
him against the jealousy or outright
negativity of others; a relationship is
putting you at risk, but you go for the
excitement and the glory of being involved; that you are a fearless warrior
in love; an alliance you have waited a

long time for finally comes together; the two of you win a case you have been fighting for together for some time; a man who may be an enemy to you and who puts you in jeopardy; you being passionate and confident in love; being incredibly happy in a long-standing balanced relationship; finding the man of your dreams; establishing a union with a partner who shares your values; finding true love with your ultimate soul mate.

Seven of Wands: Forcing yourself to stay with a man whom you have fallen out of love with or to whom you are no longer physically attracted; in your heart you want to give a relationship up, but you cannot because you are bound to the man by duty or loyalty; you must get yourself ready to go all out for a guy and put every ounce of your energy into making a relationship work; giving as much time as possible to a union in an attempt to make it a success; waiting to see if a relationship has the potential to grow before you end it; having to handle physical rejection when you know he cares but is not sexually attracted to you; staying positive about a union that is falling apart before your eyes; not letting him drain you or distract you from your own pursuits; having to go it alone in love.

Eight of Wands: A man is moving way too fast in his pursuit of you, and this frightens you a bit; him being extremely anxious to get the relationship off the ground; you know that it is too soon to come together or to move in with him, but you go ahead and move forward anyway; conditions are not right for you two to have the freedom to fully enjoy the intense passion you feel for each other; because he feels certain of his feelings for you he acts impulsively; time seems warped when you are together, as though you both exist out of time and reality; your heart and stomach flutter at the thought of him; both of you are dying to have sex with the greatest possible urgency; suddenly traveling to see each other; having no time to think as a relationship rapidly unfolds; feeling extreme panic because you do not know how to proceed with a guy; being taken by surprise in love when an old friend tells you he has always been in love with you or a new man appears in your life out of the blue.

Nine of Wands: A strong, unbreakable bond exists between two people whom nobody can tear apart; more work is needed to create a formidable relationship that cannot be undermined by the forces of society; having extreme confidence sexually with men; having good health and a positive attitude; worrying that his defenses may be too strong to break through; your passionate nature has reached a level of permanent stability and great force; not allowing a partner to attack you in any way; maintaining your own beliefs even if your man differs in his opinions; supporting your man and standing behind him no matter what troubles befall him; your enjoyment of a union is delayed until the time is right for you to come together; he is stalling for time for reasons of his own; having to physically inhibit your desire.

Ten of Wands: Your feelings for him are overwhelming; you have reached a point of overload in your current stage with him and cannot go any further; the burden of love; knowing that starting a relationship will lock you into myriad responsibilities that will make you accountable for his career, family, or social commitments; that the union demands you do service for him and others, as unpleasant as this may seem at the time of the reading; achieving a comfortable balance in sharing life tasks; feeling oppressed by your relationship; romantic maturation that allows you to establish trust in one another; being ready for the responsibility of marriage.

Page of Wands: A person who is loyal to the end in his own way; passion and adoration being directed at you by a shy but well-meaning admirer; a cheerful and active man who is always ready to go off and do things with you; staying true to the person with whom you are currently involved; being restless for new experiences that for some reason your man cannot share; one or both of you being faithful for perhaps the first time in your lives; you are anxious to move away from a guy you are committed to; a man who teaches you new ideas that inspire you creatively; having to play the role of tag-along in the social life of your partner; openly expressing your admiration and affection for another; falling in love with someone because of his ideals or moral principles; staying detached but friendly during a rough period in a relationship; enjoying the companionship of a man; making the happiness of your partner your main concern.

Queen of Wands: You are being too demanding or not demanding enough; a man inspiring you to be creative, shine socially, overcome all your fears, and enjoy life to the fullest; applying yourself to your work with confidence and brilliance; wanting to have it all with a man; dying to share your intensely passionate nature with another; craving to be noticed and to have everyone look at you; being eternally cheerful in the face of adversity; being comfortable with your strength as a woman; being aggressive for the sake of the relationship or on behalf of your man; your foot-in-mouth disease is alienating you from your partner; helping your man to be the best he can be; being extremely loyal to those you love; being a feminist in a patriarchal world.

Knight of Wands: Him fighting his feelings for you; one or both of you leaving as a solution to stagnation in a relationship; him running away so he does not have to confront his emotions; him being sexually attracted to you but fleeing out of fear of intimacy; one of you ending the relationship or leaving your current residence because you cannot handle the relationship anymore; wanting to tell him to get lost; his hiding the truth from you by not telling you his feelings; that you are too much of a challenge for him emotionally, and he cannot deal with you because of this; avoiding responsibility and commitment in love; he feels that a relationship would limit his personal freedom; a man who physically leaves you; placing sex above love in your romantic value system; trying to avoid impulsiveness in your relationships; a short-lived passion; preferring empty, casual unions with members of the opposite sex; your partner is challenging you to the extent that you must end the alliance.

King of Wands: A distant but supportive man increases your self-confidence; questioning whether he is or is not yours; deciding if he is good for you or not; he cannot give of himself completely but he is trying to do his best under difficult conditions; he tries to do the right thing with you even if that means ending the union or shifting it into a friendship; if you are involved with a man, try not to get too attached; he is trying to tell you the truth without hurting you; he picks you up each time you fall and boosts you higher; a married man who cannot be totally committed to you even if he is in love with you; an unattached man who will be monogamous; someone you can totally trust.

THE TRUMPS

The Fool: Being crazy in love with a man; following a guy you like into uncharted waters of intimacy; throwing away a secure relationship to go off with someone new who is a free spirit; total folly in your judgment of a man; acting like a complete idiot in the eyes of the world as a result of your passions; worrying that he is a gambler, a risk taker, a wanderer, or a madman; taking a chance in love; breezing through a dangerously complex romantic situation and emerging unscathed; him not wanting to appear like a fool or emotionally vulnerable; that he uses humor to express his feelings to you; the relationship follows no rules or patterns, and the man and woman make decisions about each other as they go along in life each day; a new man crosses your path when you least expect him to arrive; you have an opportunity to date someone really great, but you do not want to for some personal reason; being totally innocent and inexperienced in romance; the very first steps in what will eventually become a highly spiritual and long-term union; coincidence is a factor in how you will come together with a man; a man who does not take his relationships seriously and therefore has only short-term romances or brief affairs; ignoring the worst aspects of his behavior or serious problems in your friendship with him; avoiding being analytical about love; freeing yourself from negative karmic entanglements; a man inspires you to undergo a spiritual transformation; a man who cares not for the trappings of the material world and lives free from unnecessary possessions; adopting a wait-and-see attitude toward a new relationship.

The Juggler:
(or Magician or Magus)

Trying to figure out what his secret is; a tricky guy; a man with many ideas and the wherewithal to make them reality; one who is not verbal about his plans or his feelings; one who holds out forever until his strategy works even if he sees that you are squirming with impatience; a man who does not trust others, especially women; he directs calculated nastiness at the one he loves; he knows there is complete telepathy between you and him; he indulges in lying and game-playing; his mercurial personality is a problem; you juggle family, career, and social life without having time for much else; being extremely private and close-mouthed about your feelings for a man; being manipulative or twisting the truth to capture a man for yourself; beginning to control your own life after leaving behind a guy who was domineering; utilizing unseen forces to move the relationship forward; being extremely choosy about the men you go out with; reaching a high point of optimism and confidence in how you approach romance.

Juno:
(the High Priestess or Female Pope)

Your feelings for him are beyond the realm of logic; not being verbal about your love for a man and knowing there is wisdom in your inhibition; believing in your heart that a relationship will work out if it is meant to be; you are the older, more mature soul in a partnership; there is an unspoken psychic bond between you and him; a man who has trouble letting his woman introduce him to true spirituality; trusted intuitions and readings inform you of the arrival of a man or tell you what is really going on in an existing alliance; receiving images and other details of future relationships through your dreams and visions; staying on track when you are toughing it out with him; when apart from him, you just know what he is going through; utilizing your instincts about a man no matter how he appears to be in reality; meeting someone who shares your views on life; experiencing a relationship with a man that is purely cosmic; not overintellectualizing what is happening in a love affair and instead just letting it unfold naturally; listening to your own inner voice when trying to make a decision about whether to continue going out with someone or to sever the connection; spontaneously being aware of past lives you have shared together and knowing what roles you played for each other then.

The Empress: Being seen by your man as the source of life itself; being the muse behind all his inspired ideas and creations; promoting joy and vitality in his life; nurturing his people and his work on every level; being a wife, mother, or soul mate in your union with a man; feeling maternal instincts due to your love of a man; the matter of when you two will start a family; becoming more domesticated as a result of your living arrangement with a man; holding yourself in the highest esteem no matter what any man thinks of you; being creative in all that you do and in your approach to all your relationships; being imaginative in love; making fun out of the most routine daily tasks for him and your children; you must come up with good ideas about how to work out the problems you share; him having a good attitude toward women in general; a man who adores or even worships women; with his touch you are sexually healed; his influence makes you grow from girlhood to true womanhood; enjoying sensuality on a new level with him; a man who opens you up sexually for the first time; being a strong mature woman in how you approach your relationships with men; being ready to totally commit yourself for life to your soul mate; being his ideal mate or the woman of his dreams; coming to understand your true worth as a woman; enjoying your femininity.

The Emperor:　Trying to establish order in the home; stability in your love life helping you to organize your professional activities; having a rock-solid partnership; he has to figure out how to constructively merge your lives; working hard on a relationship until you both get it right; a long-term marriage; the appearance of your soul mate, lifetime partner, or husband; having an affair with an older man or one who is married; getting involved with someone who is a father figure to you; he acts with the full maturity of the Emperor; there is hope a youthful guy you are involved with will grow up and become a real man; a man coming through for you in a major way; a sophisticated or prestigious man whom you greatly admire will enter your life; he realizes it is high time he graduated to manhood; sensing that he needs time to be emotionally ready for a serious monogamous union; if you get together with the Emperor, you will be challenged to take on the most important relationship of your life; a man who helps you professionally by giving you good advice or introducing you to the right people; the arrival of the man you have been waiting for and whose image you have always carried in your mind and heart; becoming aware of the nature of your ideal male archetype; a man who is always there for you and on whom you can totally depend.

Jupiter:
(the Pope, Priest, or Hierophant)

Lessons learned in past relationships must be assimilated into your awareness of your current relationship; having to train the man and teach him how to love in the highest sense; being philosophical about romance; knowing that your minds are tuned into the same wavelength; spiritual marriage; just being together activates emotional education and exploration for you both; someone is coming to show you the way to the highest principles of love; you may have to coach him on how to satisfy your needs; meeting a man at your place of worship or through mutual metaphysical interests; falling in love with a man because of the beauty of his soul; a transcendental union where the relationship itself is the teacher educating both souls; having an eternal karmic bond with another; you are willing to wait forever until the right partner appears who is your equal in every way.

The Lovers:
(or Love)

A choice between two potential partners; choosing love over money or choosing with the heart rather than the mind; a marriage is in store for you; immediate and mutual attraction with a man; meeting someone whose romantic ideals match your own; making a lifetime commitment to another; within a minute of encountering a man for the first time you know that you will marry him or bear his children; you feel as if you are already married and do not need to make the relationship legal because the bond is already permanent; a man sees a woman for the first time and says, "This is my woman"; having a relationship that grows better over the years; being overly shy and sensitive when you are around the one you love; forming a business partnership with someone you adore; forming a union with someone whose personality is the exact opposite of yours; a happy love life making you a nicer person; having the purest desire to find someone to love; enjoying a traditional courtship that a man is extending to you.

The Chariot: Being aware that everything you are going through emotionally is for a purpose, whether or not you believe it at the time of the reading; a union that is meant to be; destiny placing you in the path of your soul mate; a relationship is moving too quickly for you to ascertain the value of what is happening; trying not to worry about whether your intense focus on your personal life is detracting from your work, as you will resume your professional responsibilities in due time; taking control of your own romantic fate; knowing that you cannot rush a man into making a decision about a relationship with you; while you are waiting for a man, continue to enjoy your life and do not get completely discouraged; you will meet a great guy when the time is right and no sooner; you need to take a journey by yourself and use the distance to consider what is happening with a particular man; keeping your eyes and ears open to gather information about someone you are attracted to; being absolutely sure that you want a certain man; seeing how all previous relationships have formed a path to your one true soul mate; accepting the fact that there is no compatible man available to you at the time of the reading; trusting that the right person will literally arrive on your doorstep when you are ready for him.

Justice: Legal marriage; divorcing or dissolving a partnership; your deepest desire is to find your equal; learning to trust a man; being completely satisfied as a woman in your current romantic arrangement; you can be sure that all misunderstandings with him will be straightened out; the imbalances in your behavior and in his need to be adjusted; working out past karma through a relationship and trying hard to avoid creating more problems for yourself later on; a connection based on karmic reenactment of roles you played together in past lives; re-creating the traumas of your childhood through your behavior in your relationships; knowing you must get equal respect from a man or the alliance cannot possibly go anywhere; working hard to become a better, more loving partner.

The Hermit: Striking out on your own without him; wanting more independence in a relationship; seeking privacy or solitude from him and his life; you need to branch out from working with a man and find your own career; not wanting to share your life with another because you cannot handle the emotional conflagration a relationship often sets off; not wanting to be with any man for a period of time or for the rest of your life; you are nunlike or a virgin; your attitude toward men is old-fashioned and pure of heart as you wait until the perfect man appears for you; you and he need time alone to search your souls and discover whether the union is really right for both of you; having a private place you can retreat to in order to meditate upon what is happening in your love life; climbing back into your shell as you withdraw emotionally from him because you cannot stand the relationship anymore; a monklike guy who has no women in his life; telling the truth to a man or his coming clean to you; learning to live on your own after a separation from a man; being prepared to move on if your man cannot live up to your standard of perfection; someone who is sexually celibate or introverted.

The Wheel of Fortune: A particular man or relationship is lucky for you; a person who brings wealth or opportunity to you; your friendship with him enables you to do new exciting things and enter a wonderful phase of your life; fortunate things are happening for you both that were completely unexpected; you need to lighten up and enjoy your time together instead of being weighed down by your problems; much more happiness and good times lie ahead for you both; winning a lottery of sorts together; knowing in your hearts that you are lucky and that you have it all because you have each other; seeing the ups and downs and highs and lows of relationships as a reality factor; things go well financially for you or him and this improves your attitude toward each other; sticking with him when he suffers through a losing streak; everything going your way in love; an easy relationship with a man that does not require much effort on your part.

Strength:
(or Force or Fortitude)

You both have personal problems that need to be worked out before the relationship can go any further; one or both of you need to physically clean out from intoxicants; getting healthy and adopting a clear positive attitude about your involvement with each other; two people who help each other get psychologically clean of negative thought patterns; being the braver one in a partnership and therefore being better prepared to take risks in love and life; if the two of you break up, you will recover sooner than he will; for the relationship to work out, you will be forced to give up bad habits so you can look good, feel good, and process all the emotions—positive and negative—that true love compels you to experience; one of you needs to grow up; he is your greatest supporter and the rock of your existence; being courageous in love.

The Hanged Man: Giving a relationship up; moving away from a stagnant lifestyle that you share with your man; the end of a phase in your romance where you are ready to move on to a deeper level of involvement; you will have to make a total sacrifice for him;

putting yourself out on a limb so a union can survive; surrendering to the truth of a relationship; making a complete commitment to each other based on the choices of your souls; to love another out of a sense of loyalty or duty; saying good-bye to a man whose romantic ideals are incompatible with your own; someone is going to have to compromise if the relationship is to work; having to give up someone or something that is precious to you because your man does not approve of or feel comfortable with your involvement; your total dedication to another person enables you to rid yourself of all your selfish ways; becoming capable of offering unconditional love to a man as a result of sympathetic wisdom.

Death: A relationship is putting you through dramatic experiences that are transforming you forever; his influence is inspiring you to get healthier, and you will therefore undergo physical changes; you know your arrangement with him has to be restructured from the ground up or it will certainly die; you are devastated by the loss of someone you love dearly, but ultimately his or her departure will accelerate your personal growth, even if you cannot see it at the time of the reading; a relationship that is undergoing complete renewal; death to your antiquated concept of love; knowing that your involvement with another will influence you for the better, but that this adjustment cannot be forced by either party; finding no joy in life and feeling dead inside because he is gone.

Temperance: Seeing a relationship in a clear, balanced light; you need to cool out and calm down to get a true view of what is happening between you; sticking with a man in an attempt to work out the problems you are having; time needs to pass to heal both your wounds and his; you need to wait out a stretch of time until you are both ready for the relationship; his connection with you will challenge him to straighten out the chaos and insanity in his life; a man who is prepared to wait forever if necessary for his soul mate to arrive or for you to finally fall in love with him; knowing how to be patient with grace and dignity until he comes around; he goes from one extreme to another in his feelings for you, and his mood swings undermine your confidence in him; becoming a whole person through your involvement with him; you need to balance your own behavior before you will really be ready to deeply love another; painful memories from bad past relationships fading from your consciousness; a delay before you can see him again.

The Devil: One of you has big doubts about your alliance; you are being unrealistically negative in your attitude toward him and are not seeing him the way he really is; getting depressed over romantic troubles or loneliness; both of you must clean up your act and rid yourselves of bad, debilitating habits; selfish meddling people must be ejected from your collective environment as they are causing conflict in your relationship;

discovering that his basic sexual orientation is autoerotic or pornographic; trying not to listen to the bad things people tell you about him; he is being sucked into the glamour and illusion of how society presents womankind, and therefore he has difficulty recognizing true love when it comes along; conquering your jealousy of other women; getting rid of a guy who is not good for you; being affected by his bad moods; an ignorant couple caught in hell together who cannot be intimate until they are angry at each other; him blaming all his problems on you; seeing his dark side; witnessing the evil in broken men; he is carrying a destructive relationship from his childhood into his love life as an adult.

The Tower:
(or House of God)

Figuring out that what he says is only a reflection of his fear of intimacy and not his true feelings if he tells you he does not love or need you; total chaos in a relationship where nobody is in charge or knows what is going on; being emotionally devastated over a romance gone bad; fearing that he is not the person you thought, when you learn how he kept the truth hidden from you; realizing that your partnership is not working out as you hoped it would; the masks you have worn for each other are taken off, and the lies you told each other are exposed to the light of day; you are shocked by the arrival of a man who comes along when you least expect him; the relationship turns a corner as you experience a breakthrough, and you come to understand each other at last; being aware of momentous changes taking place between you; falling to pieces and entering a state of sad shock when a person you love leaves you; tragedy influencing the course of your union with another; a new alliance with a man will be happier and better than you currently expect; liberation from an imprisoning arrangement with a man; getting rid of a guy who is not really right for you so you can clear the way for a new relationship.

The Star: Seeing signs of hope that your romance will ultimately work out beautifully for both of you; viewing your dreams and visions of love in an idealistic light; knowing you and he could have the most gloriously perfect life together; as an obstacle, the Star shows that an essential and crucial element is missing from the relationship; intimacy with another grants you ecstasy beyond any pleasure you have felt before; the miracle of finding the one you were born to be partners with; expressing your mutual adoration openly and frequently; knowing that he is the one you must marry; you both know that your union extends beyond the bonds of life; having a heavenly time when you are alone with each other; thinking that he is the most beautiful man you have ever seen and getting dizzy with joy every time you look at him; not letting any negativity in his behavior diminish your positivity and your light; having a relationship with a famous man; to meet your soul mate on the astral plane or in a dream state when you have not met him yet on earth.

The Moon: Being foggy in the head and unable to analyze your feelings because of your confusion over him; a chaotic stage in a relationship where you are struggling to work out your problems; dredging up hurts from the past that surface as issues laden with great psychological conflict; facing every fear of intimacy that both of you possess; a man who puts you through his own childhood traumas by treating you the way his father treated his mother; him using you to project upon in order to process the anxieties and phobias that he needs to release if he is to become a whole, loving person; a guy who drags you into the underworld of society; a person who knows how to push your psychological buttons; confronting any secret motives you have toward each other; he encourages you to drink or take drugs and drags you down with him; his bizarre behavior has nothing to do with you but is a by-product of a life of conflict, and he needs to heal himself through therapy or by gaining an understanding of what happened to him.

The Sun: Seeing the relationship for exactly what it is; making positive plans together for a happy future; heading together to a warm, serene environment to escape from life or just to have a wonderful holiday; information surfacing about him that you were unaware of previously; complete consciousness about the nature of your union; a wordless understanding exists between you; finding the most compatible man you have ever known with whom you achieve an easy rapport; just being near him is reason enough to feel great joy; never taking each other for granted; both of you want to be together no matter what the consequences; leaving a bad environment and finding a happier place to live together; both of you are extremely sensitive and careful not to hurt each other's feelings; your love is complete unto itself and requires nothing artificial to

make it better; he is your reason for living and you are his.

Judgement: Answering the question of
whether you two will go on as a
couple or not; decisions being
made as to whether the relationship will start up or not;
reaching a major turning point
in your partnership that will
dictate the course of both your
lives; taking each other quite seriously; undergoing physical or
spiritual cleansing due to your
involvement with a particular
man; life-threatening conditions facing either him or you
that test the depths of your feelings for each other; not looking
back and judging each other on
anything that occurred in your
past before you made the commitment to be together; the relationship itself is a spiritual
initiation for you both; the union is testing you and forcing
you to expose your inner self
while standing naked, without
your personality mask or any
other form of worldly artifice;
your involvement with him
makes you go through major
soul purification and moral re-
generation; you need to end a

relationship that does not stand up to eternity.

The Universe:
(or World)

A perfectly harmonious arrangement between two lovers; how the relationship will work out in the end; good things take time, and truly serious partnerships need to develop slowly; if you know he is the ultimate man for you, savor the courtship and enjoy the dance of the soul mates, for this may happen only once in your life; your man shows up, and he looks and acts exactly as you thought he would; trying to figure out whether a man is your destiny or not; any conflicts that plague a relationship are not a waste of time but are necessary for your moral education as a soul; repeating themes of past lifetimes together and knowing you have met again for a particular purpose; he wants everything to unfold at the proper time; accepting that true love is a long road without shortcuts if you two are in for the long haul together.

PART FIVE

———— ✦ ————

*Eight Tarot Card Readings
on Love*

These shorter Tarot card readings are representative of some of the most commonly asked questions about love problems. To answer these inquiries, the spreads that contain the fewest placements can be utilized to get specific information. The Three Card Spread and the Problem/Solution spread are perfect mediums for receiving quick information from the Tarot deck. These three readings are followed by five long readings that utilize the Subject-Combination and the Grand Cross and Four Card Spread to analyze relationships between men and women. All of these spreads are described in full detail in the "Steps for a Card Reading" section of this guide.

READING ONE

Question: I just met a guy I like, and I gave him my phone number. Will he call me?

Three Card Spread

Conditions brought over from the past: The *eight of cups* in this position shows him to be a quiet and remote figure who wants to be taken seriously in all his relationships. He has never had casual or shallow affairs with women in his past, and due to his values of devotion and emotional commitment, this cup card suggests he has had few long-term unions because of his attitude toward love. He envisions his romantic life as a solitary quest for a partner who feels as deeply as he does about matters of the heart. He has been on a long hopeful journey to seek out the one true love who could become his lifetime partner.

Present conditions: The *Tower* in this spot indicates that meeting you has turned this man's world upside down. He did not expect to connect with a woman like you, and this encounter has forever changed him. The eight of cups has already established that his love life has been an emotional desert up to now, and he is shocked and surprised to have found you. He is currently undergoing a transformation in the way he views his single status, and he considers you a miracle of sorts, a catalyst for breaking down many of his antiquated concepts of womankind. He sees you as a challenge because his attitudes and habits are undergoing drastic restructuring, a process that began the moment he met you. So it can be said with great certainty that once the dust clears from his mind, he will figure out how special your connection is, especially when he looks back on his solitary past.

What will happen in the future: The *Page of swords* in this placement shows a number of different paths he will take as he pursues his interest in you. He will either call you or arrange a meeting of your mutual friends to create a reason to get together with you. He wants to observe you further and will ask around for information on you in an almost spylike fashion. He may set you up in any number of situations socially to test your behavior and to get to know you better, but he may do this in an indirect way so you are not aware of his interest in you. Your initial conversation really got through to him, and the Tower proves he is all shook up; you are unsettled as well because meeting him has brought you to life and made you feel there is hope that you could eventually meet a great guy who has serious moral values (eight of cups).

READING TWO

Question: I have not had a decent boyfriend in years, and my love life is on hold. When am I going to meet someone new?

Three Card Spread

Conditions brought over from the past: The *three of swords* in this position symbolizes the intense pain and heartbreak you have suffered in the past. Either every man you loved has left you for another, or for some practical reason you have been forced to be apart from the one you love. You have a sad romantic history and feel as though you get the short end of the stick every time you open your heart up

to another. You are extremely vulnerable emotionally due to your past experiences with men, but you
are deeply sensitive and you are lucky to have an
extraordinary depth of feeling in a world where nobody seems to care about other people, and where
relationships are often based on personal gain instead of unconditional love.

Present conditions: The *Hanged Man* in this spot indicates that you have just about given up hope of
ever meeting a compatible soul of the male variety.
Because of your commitment to the truth, you are
prepared to sacrifice almost everything in an effort
to establish a serious relationship with the right
man. You are ready to go out on a limb for love and
would be the most loyal and devoted partner any
man could have. You will not consider getting involved with anyone who does not meet your high
standards. You are searching for a man who feels as
strongly as you do, though right now you have little
hope of meeting such a person.

What will happen in the future: The *two of swords* in
this position tells you to keep the faith and stay true
to yourself, attributes which are also associated with
the Hanged Man. Your challenge in the days ahead
will be to retain your intense belief that the right
man will enter your life when the timing is correct.
Until that time all you can do is learn how to be
satisfied as a woman on your own emotionally and
stay cool mentally about not having a man. You
need to develop a way of thinking that will serve
you in your unwavering belief that you, like every
person on this planet, have a complementary soul
who would love you if he could only find you.

READING THREE

Question: I have been going out with a guy for five years, and he wants to marry me and raise a family together. What should I do?

Problem/Solution Spread

Problem: The *Queen of wands*, the *Empress*, the *six of swords*, and the *Lovers*. This combination of cards in the problem position indicates that you are a strong and independent woman who is fully confident in her creative and social abilities (Queen of wands and the Empress). You have established an easy communicative relationship with this man (six of swords), which is probably why your alliance has lasted so long. He adores you just the way you are and is proud to have you as his woman, and he loves to show you off because you enhance his self-image. He considers you the woman of his dreams, and the Empress shows his desire to marry you and create a family together. The Lovers trump is the card of intense mutual attraction and earthly marriage and emphasizes that your physical chemistry is really strong and could grow in intensity in the years ahead. The Lovers card also symbolizes the choice you must make about whether or not to accept his proposal. The six of swords implies that this will be easy for you to do because the two of you are so compatible, and you should feel free to discuss your fears or doubts with him because he is totally open to listening to you.

Solution: Ace of swords, ace of wands, ten of cups, and the *Universe.* This combination of cards tells you that your answer is to say yes with all the power inherent in the aces of sword and wand. You know he truly loves you and wants you to be happy and fulfilled (the Empress), so you can make your decision with all the certainty and solidity of the ace of swords. The ace of wands says that married life will be a new beginning in your union and will change the nature of your current arrangement. Your commitment to each other will enhance your mutual passion for life, and both of you will rise to new heights of inspiration and creativity. The ace of wands also suggests that he wants to get you pregnant immediately. The ten of cups shows that you two will have an extremely happy home life and will find great joy in raising children together. This ten also shows that your love for each other is a bond that will not be easily broken, and this should make you both feel emotionally se-cure about your impending marriage. You have it all as a couple because you have each other, and his love makes you a complete human being; you are never in doubt about his acceptance of you as you are, with all your faults. The Universe trump only adds to the notion that he is the man you were in-tended to be with, so you can go ahead and say yes because he is your destiny and your lifetime com-panion on the long road of love.

Lesson: Page of wands and the *six of disks.* The fiery Queen of wands finds it hard to be faithful to one man, but the Page of wands shows monogamy to be the test for you in this union. You should not carry on behind his back, though you may be

tempted over the years because you naturally attract
attention from the opposite sex. You must remain
loyal to him or you could run the risk of losing the
happy family life you will establish shortly after
your marriage. You must stay true to him and make
his happiness your main concern because he wants
to do the same for you. The six of disks indicates
that you must learn how to share your lives in the
most practical sense. You must learn to take from
each other only what is fair, merge your financial
resources, and give of yourself emotionally without
hesitation. You must support each other and push
each other to succeed with endless generosity of
spirit.

READING FOUR

This reading was given to a female who has the
Queen of cups as her significator. She is an extremely busy and talented professional who rarely
has time to date. Her major concern was whether
she would meet a suitable man at any time in the
future and how long she would have to wait for a
man to arrive in her life with whom she could enter
into a compatible relationship and eventually raise
a family. The subject-combination for her reading
was Love and Partnership and Work and Business.

The Grand Cross

Your *self card* is *Temperance*. This shows that you
are desperately trying to balance the work and love
areas of your life. You are currently in a period of
gestation regarding your work. You are waiting

very patiently and trying to be level-headed as you move forward slowly but surely in your career. The same attitude carries over into the love area of your life. You are undergoing a process of smoothing out the rough edges of your personality; you are so wrapped up in your work that you might not recognize your soul mate if he strolled into your office tomorrow morning. You seem to have an innate wisdom about postponing any potential affair until conditions are right in your life and you have time for a relationship. You need the emotional solitude you are now experiencing, and it appears as though you need this time without a man to worry about so you can mentally sort out the reasons behind all of the failed romances you have had thus far.

Your *present environment* is the *Queen of disks*. This emphasizes that your main concern right now is getting together the material aspects of your existence so you can achieve financial security independently of any man. You are recognized by others for your abilities as a worker, and you are pursuing the most commercial path regarding your creative output or the sort of employment you have chosen. While you are waiting out the time period of Temperance, you remain content with your lot in life and continue to be positive and generous with other people by offering your assistance and good advice whenever you can. People look to you for support and consider you an expert on how to get things done efficiently and with great perfection. Right now you are grounding yourself in the practical realities of your world and are growing stronger and more capable as a worker each day.

Your *obstacle* is the *King of cups*. This quite simply points out that any serious relationship would be an obstacle to you right now. You must put your time and energy into taking care of your own responsibilities as the Queen of disks and continue to prepare yourself for the arrival of your lifetime partner (Temperance). Though in your heart you know romance is not pertinent to the current focus of your life, still you hunger for a man to share your existence with. The King of cups may be a powerful man in your sphere at work. You are emotionally drawn to this man, but you could never openly express your attraction to him because he is someone with whom you have to negotiate, or perhaps he is your employer. He might also be someone who has to travel for business or who lives in another part of the country or world. You are aware of your feelings for this man, but as the King of cups, he probably does not have time for a relationship right now as he is very busy taking care of business. If he feels love for you, you can be sure he is holding back a great deal of emotion; therefore his feelings would be difficult for you to read from his actions or words.

Your *hope and dream* is the *eight of cups*. This shows you being seriously devoted to your dream of having a relationship with someone who shares your moral values. Your greatest hope is that you will eventually connect with a man who is worthy of your dedication and who appreciates you for what you are, not just for who you are as the Queen of disks. You cherish a deep desire to find a lifetime partner who will satisfy the yearnings of your soul, and to this end you direct all your efforts toward

the day when such a man will come into your life.
You want only the most highly evolved union based
on trust, faith, and mutual nurturing.

Your *difficulty in the past* is the *eight of swords*. This
shows that you have experienced an amazing break-
through from a conditioned, imprisoning, and over-
intellectual state of being that has warped your
attitude toward love. Your strength in the future lies
in your newfound mental freedom and your deter-
mination never to return to having alliances with
men who hold you in a position of emotional bond-
age. All of your failed romances have actually pre-
vented you from making major mistakes that would
cost you dearly later in life by causing you to be
paired with a man who is not right for you. The
eight of swords can also signify your inability thus
far to communicate your feelings openly to the King
of cups individual who is your current obstacle in
both love and work, the subject-combination of this
reading.

Your *last of the present* is the *nine of wands*. This indicates that you have arrived at a point where your
passionate nature is strong and confident. You are
not going to be pushed around easily or dominated
by any man no matter how much you love him. You
are aware of the delays that have plagued your love
life thus far, especially now that the eight of swords
is liberating you from a time without a relationship,
and Temperance is currently preparing you for the
arrival of your perfect partner. Your strength has
gotten you through the lonely isolation of the eight
of swords, and you have learned how to control
your feelings until the right person comes along

(eight of cups). You have been protected from any superfluous or premature involvements. The King of cups is your obstacle, and this shows that not having a man in your life is bothering you. But because you are willing to hold out for a happy marriage with another (eight of cups) and are fully prepared to wait (Temperance), you will be able to recognize a formidable partner when he enters your life.

Your *first of the future* is the *nine of swords*. This signifies that you are anxious about any neglect you may have suffered in the past and shows you will reach a time when you will dwell on the worst aspects of your loveless existence. You will feel burned out by the long eight of swords coma and find yourself awash in self-pity and feeling all alone in the world. Though as the Queen of disks you selflessly give to everyone, you will agonize over whether anybody would give you equal support. Unkind attitudes or words projected at you by others will get under your skin perhaps for the first time. There may be misunderstandings at work, perhaps with the King of cups whom you so greatly admire, and this will make you feel awful. There is a period ahead of sleepless nights when you restlessly go over conversations in your mind in an attempt to understand what is really going on with him.

Your *future environment* is *Judgement*. This implies a major decision being made by you or another in the days ahead. That decision will directly affect your destiny. You may become aware that a man with whom you were once involved has suddenly come to his senses and realized that you are the woman for him, or perhaps the King of cups man will become a serious issue you must come to terms with. Either way, this trump shows you reaching a crucial turning point when you will be forced to see things exactly as they are. Though you may suffer in silence (nine of swords), you will ultimately grow stronger by accepting the truth of the situation. You may be forced to take on new roles or a new way of life in the days to come. This may mean moving into a totally different arena at work or in romance.

Your *outer influence* is *the Emperor*. This portends the appearance of a mature and financially secure man in your life. This man has the power to move mountains for you and can help you gain professionally by giving you good advice or introducing you to the right people. After you encounter him and recognize him as the Emperor, he will become the most important person in your life. The Emperor and the King of cups may be the same man coming through for you in a major way in the days ahead, but currently this person is an obstacle to you in the areas of love and work. You will totally identify with his personality as he will encompass a male archetype that is close to your heart. You will find him easily understandable, totally attractive, and everything you have ever wanted in a man. He will be a father figure who will protect you and always be there for you when you need him.

Your *hope and fear* is the *Knight of cups*. This symbolizes your fear that any offers of love and pleasure from the King of cups/Emperor character will be empty and mean nothing in reality. The Knight of cups is a man who does not know exactly what he wants from a relationship or from women in general. His confusion unfortunately causes him to make hollow and meaningless promises. You will experience much anxiety (nine of swords) over whether the Emperor person who extends an invitation to you will come through in the end. You will be deeply concerned by any instability or addictive behavior problems that will become obvious to you in the future. You are sick to death of weak alliances (eight of swords and nine of wands) and only want to find a stable man who shares your deepest convictions (eight of cups) and is strong enough to be your equal in love.

Your *outcome* is *Justice*. This can indicate a legalized partnership of one form or another. Justice also shows you finally being rewarded in love after a long struggle where you never lost your moral values for one second. As a woman, you will be completely satisfied in the end and will win the prize for your wise patience (Temperance) and the selfless effort you put into all your past relationships as the Queen of disks. This involvement with the King of cups will work out in your favor, and you two will ultimately establish a fair, balanced, and healthy partnership. Any misunderstandings between you two will be worked out, and all your problems with men will be resolved; people who have treated you badly in the past will come to their senses and make amends to you.

Four Card Spread

Work and business: The *Page of wands* in this position shows that at work you are seen by everyone as a loyal, honest team player who cheerfully takes

on all tasks assigned to you. Though you are not yet
an executive, your steadfast passion for your job has
been noticed and is appreciated by the King of
cups/Emperor man. Justice as your outcome pre-
dicts that you will be rewarded for all your efforts
and that you are seen as more than capable due to
your Queen of disks persona. You must keep on
plugging away on the job so you can continue to
achieve a high level of satisfaction with your output.
No matter how romance, or the lack of it, influences
your moods, you will remain directed toward ful-
filling your responsibilities, and you will always
pursue your creative interests even when love problems distract you from reaching your highest goals
(King and eight of cups). You must always seize all
opportunities that are offered to you professionally,
as this is how you will forever retain the excitement
and inspiration that make you such a wonderful
person to be involved with at work.

Love and partnership: The Devil in this placement
shows you are undergoing heavy testing in the love
area of your life. You have learned how to leave
behind negative partners who dragged you down
in one way or another, and you are trying to overcome all the painful emotions that stem from your
interest in the King of cups. You want to free yourself from a future of bad relationships with unsuit-
able people, and because you have such high morals
(eight of cups), you cannot afford to get involved
with deadbeats or unbalanced men (Knight of cups
as your hope and fear reiterates this issue). Your
strong desire to have a workable relationship with
a man is greater than the reality that nobody is cur-

rently available or interested in you who meets your high standards. You need to let go of all of your weakest emotions such as jealousy, obsession, and possessive behavior to reach a point of being comfortable with your lot in life whether you are with a man or not. In all your romantic interludes to come, your intentions must be clear and your desires pure, even if the man you are involved with acts like the Knight of cups or worse.

Trouble and conflict: The *Knight of swords* in this placement signifies that every man you have been involved with has been too busy pursuing his career goals to have time to really get to know you. You have thus far chosen selfish men who are too wrapped up in themselves to share their lives with anyone, no matter how devoted or fantastic the woman may be. These men are so petrified of intimacy and of delving into the frightening realm of emotional growth that they remain unattached so as to avoid exposing themselves to potential moments of vulnerability. The Knight of swords guys cannot bear the thought of having a highly devoted relationship with a woman, which all men eventually seek in their hearts once they have sorted out why they feel so inadequate subconsciously when life has treated them badly.

Money and material matters: Juno in this placement shows that you must begin to utilize your feminine intuition both at work and in all your relationships with men in the days to come. You must learn to trust yourself and get comfortable with the fact that you know more about what is going on than any of your co-workers do. Taking this crucial step will increase your self-confidence (nine of wands) and strengthen your professional reputation as someone who always offers her opinion, no matter how far-fetched it may seem to others. As far as money goes, you must have faith that it will come to you as a result of your Queen of disks/Page of wands role, and Justice as your outcome ensures that you will have total success in the end. Do whatever you must to use your senses beyond the realm of logic, and listen to any psychic types who give you readings, for they are telling you exactly what you need to know in order to proceed financially and make the most of your talents. You are more mature and have greater wisdom than those around you, and your understanding of people is your trump card professionally and will be romantically.

READING FIVE

This reading was given to a female who has the Queen of cups as her significator. She had recently fallen madly in love with a man she had just met. They were both involved in the same profession and seemed to have just about everything in common. They exchanged phone numbers after their initial meeting, and she wondered if she would hear from him or whether she should call him and make the first move. She wanted to know more about him and requested specific information on his personality and overall romantic history. Her subject-combination was double Work and Business.

The Grand Cross

Your *self card* is *the Wheel*. This extremely lucky trump makes you feel as though your life right now is too good to be true as your wildest dreams become real in the context of your daily life. This man you have just met has fueled your happiness to an amazing degree. Even professionally he is a positive factor that can only enrich your outer world destiny. You can see how there will be more encounters with him in the future no matter who makes the first move and calls the other to get together again. No matter what path the relationship takes, you are experiencing the best time of your life thus far; meeting him is your destiny, and you know it. Even if you never see each other again, you will always be glad you were in the right place at the right time to encounter such a person. You will always be grateful for the fantastic time you had together and for all the wonderful ideas and emotions he has inspired in you. This potential romance would be an easy one for you emotionally and would only boost your confidence and enjoyment of life. The Wheel also suggests that neither of you ever expected to meet such a compatible person, and this whole experience has taken you both by surprise.

Your *present environment* is the *five of wands*. This proves that both of you were deeply affected by your first encounter. Already you are passionately entwined even though you have not yet spoken of your feelings. He is crazy about you, so with great certainty you can pursue the relationship with all your energy. You should not think logically about what next step either of you should take to approach each other. Your common interests were part of the immediate bond forged between you and will serve to bring you closer together. You are the sort of people who fervently follow your hearts because you care about the world and feel that your destiny is to leave behind good works as opposed to more problems. You are also trying to come to terms with your true feelings for him, and you are mentally testing yourself to see whether you want to take the risk of calling him. The physical chemistry that exploded the moment you met is real and mutual. You would go to the ends of the earth for each other, and you would fight for causes you believe in to the depths of your souls.

Your *obstacle* is the *five of swords*. This signifies that something is blocking you mentally and shows you repeating your initial conversation over and over in your mind. You are trying to make up your own mind no matter what anyone around you says about this being a potentially serious relationship for you. With the five of wands and the Wheel, all you have to do is follow your heart and reach out to him without fearing that he'll be too busy to speak to you or that he will not be interested in you. Your synchronicity with him proves that as a couple you two would be able to move your union forward without any advice from others. You desperately want to talk to him again, and you really should not listen to what anyone else tells you to do. Your obstacle is that the romantic problems of other people have nothing to do with the bond between you and him. You can hold your own intellectually against any opposing opinions offered to you, and you need to move away from the members of your usual social circle on whom you have depended for advice in the past.

Your *hope and dream* is the *ace of wands*. This shows that, regardless of any man, you want to start over in some area of your life. You envision a different daily existence than you currently have, and your encounter with this man has only strengthened your desire to move on to new territory or to strike out in a different direction creatively. The five of wands is the driving force behind these feelings; you passionately want to express to him everything inside you. The Wheel as your self card only adds to your ability to see into the future with great clarity and optimism, and you are ready to begin a romance with him regardless of what anyone says to discourage you or to extinguish your intense love for him. You want to begin a relationship with him more than anything else, and you need to make an effort to let him know you care. You are going crazy because you crave a physical union with him, and you can be completely confident that he feels wild emotions when he thinks of you. The five of swords pressure is the only block preventing you from building a future together.

Your *difficulty in the past* is the *Page of disks*. This says that your struggle all along has been to become self-sufficient and to hold your own materially. In your past relationships, you had to make all the practical adjustments and shoulder the burden for the couple as a unit. You have been working very hard, and in the future you will have to continue to apply yourself with the utmost diligence to your professional responsibilities. In your career you have always been an assistant or an apprentice, and this has been a problem because you know that you

are more than capable of running the show should
you be given a chance. Your devotion to your work
is in your favor, especially with the Wheel as your
self card. The only difficulty here arises from your
preoccupation with your work; you have avoided
lasting romantic connections, but only because none
of your past boyfriends were worth the effort. They
were not good enough for you, and they were not
as serious about the relationship as you were.

Your *last of the present* is *the Chariot*. This placement shows that you are aware that everything you
have ever gone through emotionally for better or for
worse has prepared you for your relationship with
this man. Destiny put you in the path of this person,
and your physical placement in or movement into
his sphere was meant to be. The Wheel as your self
card emphasizes this truth. If for some reason this
man is not the one for you, there is someone new
right around the corner (ace of wands as your hope
and dream) who will desire you with all the passion
(five of wands) and the optimism (the Wheel) and
the down-to-earth nature (Page of disks) that you
currently possess. You know that your journey to
your intended partner is taken care of, and the Chariot proves that this issue has not troubled you except
when people have nagged you about your romantic
life (five of swords). You know in your heart that
you are exactly where you are supposed to be and
doing what you were put on earth to do, and you
have always assumed that the right man would appear at the right time when your soul development
is such that you are fully prepared for a serious relationship. You have the wisdom to know that such

a union cannot be hurried, and you always accepted the fact that no equal was available to you, so you just worked hard and developed your talents and your resources (Page of disks).

Your *first of the future* is the *Knight of cups*. This shows your concern that if you make the first move, he will make only a partial offer of his heart to you. He may ask you out on a date or arrange to get together with you, but for some reason he will behave as though he is not really deeply interested in you. You will go through a cycle of thought that revolves around whether he is unstable emotionally or under the influence or just an illusory character when it comes to love. He will be slightly confused about how to approach you, which his actions will show. He will need to figure out exactly what he wants from you, and until he does, he will appear fickle and out of control. Your awareness of this behavior will help you maintain the clear perspective that you now have with the Wheel and the Chariot.

Your *future environment* is the *ten of wands*. This expands the significance of the ace and the five of wands you have already received in this reading to the greatest level of caring for another human being that you are capable of. You will be overwhelmed by your feelings for him, and your desire will become almost a burden for you, especially in conjunction with all the work responsibilities you will have placed on your shoulders in the days to come. As you get to know him, you may adopt your usual Page of disks personality and take on his career or social commitments as though they were your own. The relationship will demand that you carry an extra load and help out with all aspects of his life, but this is part of what comes with a serious relationship. With the Chariot and the Wheel you know that you are more than ready to meet any challenges.

Your *outer influence* is the *four of swords*. This placement shows you trying to decide what to do about your feelings for him. You will retreat mentally from everyone around you so you can sort out your options and make your choices after much deliberation. You need solitude to get your mind straight. There are calm, silent days ahead during which you will reflect on the reasons why such a man would cross your path at this time and on what you should do if ultimately a friendship forms between you. You will surrender to moments of meditation and days of listening only to the workings of your inner mind if only to defeat the intrusive five of swords, which is blocking your thoughts about love. After this period passes, you will feel as though you want to get out of the house and live and experience the ace, five, and ten of wands to their most passionate heights.

Your *hope and fear* is the *Knight of wands*. This card in this placement typically signifies that your greatest fear about him is that he will turn his back on the intense feelings he obviously has for you. Though he is sexually attracted to you in the extreme, his tendency may be to flee due to a fear of intimacy or because of a previous pattern of avoiding responsibility and commitment in love. One or both of you may have to travel for work, which may also block the quick progress of your coming together, even though the Chariot proves you covered a lot of ground in your first encounter. With the Wheel and the Chariot you can be sure that if there is a delay, it will be because the timing of the relationship needs that gap so you two can meet again when the time is right. The ace of wands seems to be saying that you need to see each other again in a different place at a particular time so the union will have a chance to grow. Your current residence is not the proper atmosphere for nurturing a relationship of such intense mutual passion.

Your *outcome* is *Justice.* This shows that no matter what happens with this man, your greatest desire is to find a male counterpart who can respect you as an equal. You know you must be completely satisfied with the arrangement you eventually carve out with him or with the next man waiting around the corner. The four of swords experience in your future will help you settle any imbalanced thoughts you have about this now. Any future relationship with a man must make you feel wanted, happy, and emotionally secure. In the end, you may legally tie the knot with him or form a legal partnership of sorts, even if only on a professional level. You may also reject him if he is not willing to work out his Knight of cups/Knight of wands tendencies through his involvement with you. There will be things to struggle over with him regardless of your compatibility, but ultimately any misunderstandings will be resolved to your advantage.

Four Card Spread

Work and business: The Wheel in this spot says that luck is on your side, and something spectacular is coming your way as your career takes a dramatic upturn. This trump may also show this man helping you reach the top professionally through his personal connections or other opportunities that he will bring your way. You are fully aware of the good fortune portended by the Wheel as your self card in the Grand Cross spread, and this positive turn of events will help you get through any relationship problems that arise between you in the days ahead.

Love and partnership: The *three of disks* here signifies that both of you have come to the end of an era in the way you experience love on a practical level. His Knight of cups/Knight of wands tendencies seem to be residue from past unhappy, incompatible alliances with the wrong women. You have both worked hard in previous relationships to try to get it right, and you are prepared to stick it out when the going gets rough if you deeply desire the other person, as you two currently do (five of wands). Still there will be a need for serious reflection on your part (four of swords) before you move on to create a new life together (ace of wands) because your caring for each other will grow into the ten of wands once you both begin to think for yourselves about what sort of relationship you want to build together in the future (five of swords). Also, the three of disks says you will definitely be working together on a project no matter what becomes of your personal relationship.

Trouble and conflict: The *seven of swords* in this position continues the sword theme established with the five of swords as your obstacle in the preceding spread. The seven is also in a conflicting position and implies that the arrangement the two of you eventually decide upon will be very different from the typical societal concept of a union, even though Justice as your outcome suggests that a legal partnership will be forged between you. Even if you work or live together, you will have to allow each other the mental freedom to be yourselves and to express yourselves without fear of censure. You need to pursue new avenues and attitudes about relationships and adopt less conventional roles than you have in previous unions. You will have to be able to communicate freely without fear of losing each other; this does not seem to be happening with the wands in this reading showing your very strong desire for each other. Your life together will feature mutual independence, and though you will share many interests you must always respect each other's privacy and individuality if the relationship is to work out between you.

Money and material matters: The *King of wands* in this placement indicates that no matter what happens between you, he is a supportive man and will be a good friend to you because of his intense interest in you and your common passion for professional interests (five of wands). Even if he cannot give you his undivided attention because he is busy or not emotionally ready for a serious commitment yet (Knight of wands), he will always be honest with you and let you know exactly what he is feeling at all times even if his tendency in the past was never to let any woman know how much he cared for her. He adores you and also sees how fortunate your meeting was, and he knows his connection with you is destiny (the Wheel and the Chariot). You will ul-

timately see that he is a good person whether he is
yours in the end or whether the union is delayed
due to his hectic schedule. When he is far away, you
should have no doubt about whether you can trust
him or not because he will always tell you the truth
and also because his romantic nature is basically
monogamous. He will always be a positive force in
your personal and professional life, and he will inspire you to work hard and become a more capable
person (Page of disks) in all areas of your life.

READING SIX

This reading was given to a female who has the
Queen of disks as her significator and who was involved with a man in a serious relationship. At the
time of the reading, they had reached a stalemate
because the man seemed to be psychologically unable to make a commitment to her. He was having
trouble deciding what he wanted to do about their
alliance. She requested information from the cards
as to whether they should give up on the relationship, take a break from each other for a while, or
stay together and slog it out. She also wanted to
know what would happen if they did go their separate ways. Would they eventually come back together? If so, how long would they be apart? The
subject-combination of the reading was Work and
Business and Love and Partnership.

The Grand Cross

Your *self card* is *the Empress*. This shows you se-
renely waiting to see if this man will realize just how

wonderful you are and how willing you are to nurture him on every level. You are also biding your time until he ultimately decides whether or not to continue your romance. You are constantly loving and creative in your approach to him, and you are working hard to make all the routine tasks you share fun and exciting. You have your own set of values; you are kind and pleasant to others, no matter how badly they may behave toward you. Your sensuality and your delight in your own femininity are obvious to him, and even if he does not express his wonder at the complete woman that you are, you can be sure that he does see you as his ideal woman; in his heart he knows that the two of you could eventually establish a happy home and family life to which you would totally commit yourself.

Your *present environment* is the *eight of cups*. This indicates that your devotion to this man is intense even as you are struggling to discover whether the emotion you feel for him is the best thing for you as the Empress. Though he brings out the Empress in you and has made you feel maternal and domestic, you must seriously consider whether he is the right man for you. To this end you are trying to make a decision based on serious values. You have shown him you are devoted and are always there for him day or night. There is no doubt how much you want the relationship with him to work out because you see him as your perfect lifetime partner. The bottom line right now is whether a romantic arrangement with him will deeply satisfy you and whether he can treat you like the goddess you know yourself to be.

Your *obstacle* is *Jupiter*. In this position, the card

of true spirituality indicates that the relationship itself is a teacher to both of you. This card also reiterates the fact that this is a potentially permanent
bond and not a quick love affair. The ultimate question at this time is whether this man can come through
on the highest level, and to discover this you are seeking information from all the sources of wisdom you
can find. You are utilizing every idea about love to analyze why the romantic education of this union is important for you to experience and why his personality
affects you so powerfully. The problem here is that
you feel certain he is your soul mate, but he is having
difficulty accepting this fact. The transcendant nature
of your connection and the otherworldly chemistry
between you are hard to fit into the reality of your
lives, and this is troubling you. In your mind you
know your bond is karmic and future-oriented, and
your souls long to be together no matter what the consequences may be in your daily existence.

Your *hope and dream* is the *three of wands*. This
shows that you must keep telling him over and over
how much you care for him, even if he seems uncomfortable with your endless expressions of love.
This is the only way you can reach him, and as the
Empress you can act in no other manner. With the
serious eight of cups and the soulfully aware Jupiter, this approach is perfectly all right, because the
bond between you is obviously eternal. You are prepared to fight for the survival of the relationship if
you must, and you want to put every ounce of your
energy into creating a union that would continually
inspire you and give you a feeling of passionate security in your life. The three of wands in the hope

and dream position also says that being able to easily express yourself to your beloved is something you have always dreamed of being able to do.

Your *difficulty in the past* is *the Hermit*. This shows that both of you have been alone romantically for so long there is a mutual awkwardness about suddenly being involved with someone on a daily basis. Though both of you have spent years searching for true love based on soul compatibility, you have not yet met your soul mates, and both of you are aware of this fact. You are both analyzing your bond in the light of truth, and the eight of cups and Jupiter only add to the intense quest you are both pursuing. Both of you had your share of solitude in the past, but only because you had not met anyone you wanted to share your life with. The Hermit also suggests that in the future you may need to take a break from each other to discover whether your union can go the distance through thick and thin. Both of you are prepared to give up if your connection does not hold up to your individual standards of perfection.

Your *last of the present* is the *five of cups*. This card in this position symbolizes your disappointment in the way things have been between you and him recently. You feel as though you have gone backwards together, and an emptiness has filled your heart where there should be joy and serenity because you are the Empress in this relationship. The fire and passion that you originally felt for him has been snuffed out by tears, and you have felt sad beyond belief. This experience has prepared you for the possibility that this union will be severed, and you know that even if things do not work out, you will always love this man. The five of cups represents the ultimate challenge of friendship between lovers, just as Jupiter is the challenge of spirituality and the Hermit is the challenge of the truth or of returning to a solitary position in love. This man has had trouble cutting through his doubts and insecurities, and both of you have had difficulty breaking free from the memories of love lost in your romantic past. Nobody likes to get the five of cups in a reading about love, but it is in a past placement of the spread and suggests that unless you two are true friends, your future together does not look good.

Your *first of the future* is the *Knight of wands*. It looks as though one or both of you will be departing from your current arrangement, at least for a short period of time. He is having trouble dealing with his feelings for you, and he will continue to impulsively turn his back on what you, as the Empress, are trying to build with the total devotion of the eight of cups. Jupiter and the Hermit reiterate the specter of solitude that has been hanging over your heads, so it is obvious you need a break from the intensity of the relationship to allow you to do some thinking independently of each other. Though he loves you, his tendency is to run away, and oddly enough, as the Knight of wands his destructively fearful behavior is a by-product of his intense passion for you. As the Empress you bring him to his knees, and he wants to flee in terror each time you bring up the serious emotional issues facing you both now.

Your *future environment* is the *Page of wands*. This suggests that, even with all the conflict you are experiencing, you two will remain romantically faithful to each other whether you are physically together or apart. You have a spiritual bond that cannot be destroyed by anything on earth, and you are both aware that your destiny is to be together (Hermit and Jupiter). Other potential lovers have nothing to do with the choices you are making now, and it is obvious that no one else comes close to being a lifetime partner for either of you. You will stay friendly while you are apart. You will be his number one fan and he will be yours, no matter what.

Your *outer influence* is the *eight of disks.* This shows that your major reason for taking a vacation from the relationship is that you both have a lot of work responsibilities that have nothing whatsoever to do with your alliance. You must undergo a round of actual physical toil on a project. This will require you to be alone for a while so you can have time to get the job done properly. Also, it will take a tremendous effort to reorganize your social arrangements so that you can eventually reside together in an atmosphere that is creative and constructive for both of you. A practical arrangement needs to be established that will enable you both to take care of your individual tasks to secure your separate financial destinies. You both need to bring in more money or build up your resources so you can become a solid team in the days ahead.

Your *hope and fear* is the *two of swords.* This emphasizes that you both must keep the faith and stay certain in your hearts and minds that the relationship will work out in time. While apart you must trust each other to the core of your being and know that the problems you have had are due to material imbalances; they did not arise because you do not deeply love each other. Even though his Knight of wands behavior toward you is painful and his indecision about you is tearing you apart (five of cups), you must never doubt that he really wants things to work out between you eventually. Your greatest challenge in the days to come will be to maintain a constant vigilance over your thoughts and emotions so you can retain your faith in him. Every time you doubt his intentions you undermine his confidence that your union will grow into a permanent alliance, which is something that has eluded you both thus far.

Your *outcome* is the *three of cups*. As the wrap-up card in a reading examining love the three of cups screams out that ultimately you and this man will create a long-standing, highly evolved relationship based on a marriage of souls that just goes on and on developing beautifully for the rest of your lives. He will make up to you for the roller coaster of emotions he has put you through. The separation you will experience does not mean your friendship is over; the Page of wands ensures a loyalty that will not die. In the end you will be deliriously happy together. You will enjoy all the good things in life, and you will never take each other for granted. It is he who is having trouble coming to terms with sharing and celebrating the fruits of love with one person, but this is a major commitment for any Knight of wands to make.

Four Card Spread

Work and business is *Strength*. You are both working extra hard to eliminate the negative competitive
elements that distinguish the earliest stages of a union of such intensity of feelings. Until you both
make the life changes to bring you back together
and form a solid union (eight of disks), you both
must get rid of your personality crutches and psychological postures through understanding your
own internal mechanisms in an atmosphere of solitude (the Hermit). In terms of your career, you have
never been in a stronger position to take on new
projects or felt more capable of doing so. Your professional confidence arises from the sheer force of
your immense talent. Both the love area and the
work area of your life will benefit from your effort
to become a more powerful person and to get
through all struggles by utilizing your internal
strength. You can be confident now that you will
win backing for all your projects, and if you apply
for a new job, you will be hired immediately.

Love and partnership is the *five of cups*. This means
that this man, when faced with the soul mate relationship with his Empress whose endless love and
devotion is a dream come true, has a tendency to
kick the cup of love over so the contents are lost to
the earth forever. His unconscious desire to destroy
the relationship and to fail to come through for you
is due to his bad experiences in love where he has
been hurt by women who were not of the Empress
variety. The five of cups was also in the last-of-the

present position in the previous spread, so the disappointment and heartbreak are already evident to you. The saving grace for your partnership is the three of cups, representing the happiness you will eventually share, proving that the loss of love associated with the five is just a temporary stage. Early on in this sort of intense union a topsy-turvy state of emotions is natural and to be expected, even if it is hard for an open, loving person to bear.

Trouble and conflict is the *Page of cups*. In this position the Page of cups can be interpreted to mean that you are being too passive and perhaps too meek and gentle in dealing with this man. The discord between you has made you raw and vulnerable, and you become easily unglued by his Knight of wands behavior. You go to pieces at the thought of being without him even though as the Empress you are more than capable of going out into the world on your own, since Strength ensures your professional success. With the three of wands as your hope and dream, you should try to utilize free expression, show the rougher edges of your personality, and stop being so overly nice. You can be bolder about your wide range of feelings. Tell him the truth about your emotions (Jupiter and the Hermit) instead of swallowing your pride and playing a secondary role in the development of the relationship. Also this Page could show the difficulties you are having because he is emotionally immature and unprepared for an Empress in his life. He needs to grow slowly into the relationship, and your departure from his daily existence may hasten his growing up and help him become a real man. Also, a child, or the issue of children, may get in the way of his deciding whether to continue his involvement with you.

Money and material matters is the *Knight of wands*. This card was also your first of the future in the Grand Cross spread. It shows that you will be leaving your current environment so that the relationship can move forward. By departing from the scene of his daily life, you will force him to come to terms with the enormity of your role in his world as the Empress who is his ideal companion and ultimate soul mate. Unfortunately he needs this separation to get a clear picture of the relationship, because now he is running away from making any practical decision about how you two will work things out in reality. Sadly enough, you are making the trip alone (the Hermit), but stay positive (two of swords) and remember there is a lifetime of happiness ahead (three of cups). You both are wise enough (Jupiter and the Hermit) to realize this separation is the right thing at this time so you can eventually share a solid day-to-day existence together (eight of disks).

READING SEVEN

This reading was given to a female who has the Queen of swords as her significator. She had lived with a man for a few months. They had reached a stage in their relationship where the honeymoon had worn off, reality had begun to intrude upon their harmony, and his behavior had begun to change. Up to this point he had always been gentle with her, but now he had begun to behave in an unfriendly manner toward her, especially when she complained of the change in their romance. During the reading, she wanted to know why he was being hostile toward her when she knew he loved her. She also asked whether their union would make it through this rough period. The subject-combination of the reading was Work and Business and Love and Partnership.

The Grand Cross

Your *self card* is the *three of disks*. This shows that a major phase of activity and development has been reached in the relationship. Though you have come to agree upon practical or financial matters together, you two are still struggling to build a permanent union with a strong foundation. You consider yourselves a team, and thus far this has inspired you both to finish up all old business so you can begin to focus on how you will live your day-to-day lives as a productive unit. You may be considering a mutual project that would certainly be successful and showcase both your talents. Until you both figure out how you are going to accomplish your individual current occupational responsibilities, you must be patient. You both need to bring to completion all dangling business entanglements that are residue from your lives before you came together.

Your *present environment* is *the Universe*. This signifies that you are undergoing a major shift in your perception of this relationship. You are beginning to realize that the closest bond between two people develops slowly over time if they want a rock-solid union (three of disks). You want this man to be your partner for life, and you feel that destiny has brought you together for a particular purpose. All of the problems that you are having will ultimately lead to better conditions, as the Universe trump always implies perfection as an outcome to any dilemma. A crucial romantic education is under way that will lead to a higher level of commitment as you go out into the world independently and together.

Your *obstacle* is the *Knight of wands*. This card indicates that even with the specter of the need to work hard hanging over the relationship, and over your professional lives as well (three of disks), and despite your acknowledgment of the depth of your connection (Universe), you both have an impulsive tendency to run away from responsibility and to avoid confronting your feelings when you are in love. This Knight proves that you desire each other to the passionate core of your being, and this healthy hunger is preventing you from dealing with the more practical issues that surround the relationship (three of disks) and stopping to examine them in the most absolute sense (Universe). You need to decide whether this man's fear of intimacy is really right for you at this time or whether your intense interest in him is distracting you from your work (three of disks) and your personal soul destiny (Universe). Though you quite obviously adore each other, you both want to escape the feelings of falling forever in love, which are currently undermining the solid union you are trying to create together as symbolized by the self card and the present environment card in this spread.

Your *hope and dream* is the *Queen of swords*. This
says that if you are to achieve the goals you have
already decided upon, you must push like mad for
what you want. You need to learn to ignore problems you are having with him and continue to make
your ideas become reality whether they include him
or not. You may have to be harsher than usual in
the face of current conditions and never forget that
there will be no real growth for either of you unless
you aggressively push both yourself and him to
move forward in life. You never expected to have
the opportunity to share your existence with a man
who seems so perfectly suited to you (Universe).
You are busy redefining your assumption that you
would never find an equal here on earth and therefore would be alone without love, a typical interpretation of the Queen of swords in a reading that
focuses on love.

Your *difficulty in the past* is *the Sun*. This tells you
that the difficulty all along has been whether you
see the relationship clearly or not and whether you
can maintain a positive outlook about it while you
two are sorting out what is important to your mutual happiness and contentment. You are busy
strengthening the connection between you (three of
disks). You want this partnership to be the ultimate
one for you and the end of the line in terms of your
romantic history (Universe). The serenity that you
two could experience together has eluded you thus
far, and there has been some confusion in your mind
as to whether you want to stay with him or not. In
the future you two need to spend more time alone
together so you can move forward with greater

awareness and consideration of your true personalities. For now all you can really do is speak the
truth about your feelings so both of you can get past
the defensive Knight of wands posturing you are
relying on, as it is preventing both of you from
growing into greater consciousness through the
friendship you have already established.

Your *last of the present* is the *nine of wands*. You
two have reached a point where you are standing
on solid ground, especially in conjunction with the
three of disks and the Universe. You have made a
passionate commitment because you are wild about
each other (Knight of wands and the Sun), and you
want to create a union that will support and protect
both of you against anyone or anything that threat-
ens to undermine your mutual desire for a workable
partnership. You have also realized that you must
continue to maintain your own beliefs and goals
(Queen of swords) even if he disagrees with you
about which way the relationship should go, especially if he has been stalling for time while he gets
up the courage to deal with his love for you in a
confident and mature manner rather than as the
Knight of wands.

Your *first of the future* is the *five of disks*. This says
that you must simplify the life-style you have shared
thus far; otherwise both of you will worry about
money in the days ahead. With the three of disks, the
Universe, and the Sun as your foundation, you know
that financial problems cannot ruin what you already have between you. You may, however, lack the
funds to experience good times together (the Sun);
this certainly will influence the direction your union

takes in the future. Also, the monetary needs of others around you may detract from your ability to be more freewheeling on a material level and to have more fun together, especially with the taskmaster three of disks in the lead position of the spread.

Your *future environment* is *the Lovers*. This shows that you will make a choice as to whether to continue the relationship or give up on it because of the challenges that face you now. Though you have a fabulous physical compatibility, the five of disks suggests that money problems or practical considerations are preventing the sun from shining on you both. In the future your passion for each other will continue, and the initial attraction that brought you together in the first place will not go away easily (Universe). No matter what takes place in reality, your bond will remain strong and unbreakable, and you will continue to be behind each other one hundred percent. You will also discuss the matter of marriage in the days ahead.

Your *outer influence* is the *ace of swords*. This brings your intellectual clarity to a point when you will simply know that the relationship will work out ultimately. You need to decide if this man is worth all the effort, and if so, you must go for it with all your power and drive. You are already struggling to make this decision, and the Lovers trump only reemphasizes this fact. Your families and friends may deeply influence the way this union will proceed. If others cause problems between you, try to look at the bright side, and then come up with a complete plan as to how you will both handle your arrangements with others so you can accomplish the tasks required (three of disks) for this alliance to move forward with renewed strength and vigor (nine of wands).

Your *hope and fear* is *the Hermit*. This tells you that problems will arise from the issue of how to preserve your privacy and individuality without losing yourself (Queen of swords, too) as you focus intensely on love matters in the days ahead. You are worried that when your mind is clear enough to finally see the truth of what is happening (the Sun), you will realize there will always be more conflicts to fight together. In conjunction with the five of disks, this trump reiterates the suggestion that you simplify your lives on the material level so that both of you can do the work required of you (three of disks). One of you may be hiding either wealth or poverty from the other (five of disks). This fact will come to light in the future (Hermit and Sun), and this may lead you both to do some soul-searching to decide whether this union can survive, but all the passion and love between you will never be questioned.

Your *outcome* is the *King of swords*. This prepares you for the likelihood that this man will show himself to be a demanding, controlling, or authoritative person who feels he has to make all the decisions for both of you because he thinks that he knows best. You are probably already aware of this quality in him, even though early in a relationship both people try to appear kind and unchallenging to each other. He will eventually seem harsh to you, but as the Queen of swords who relentlessly pursues her own goals, you are more than a match for him. As he challenges you to see things his way, he will become a catalyst for your discovery of new ideas that you will utilize in your work or in future relationships. His personality will be a teacher to you and will help you break down all your brittle and ancient concepts of love. This factor will help you shatter the false mind-set of lofty ideals you have held in your heart about love (Hermit and Lovers). His views on romance are unusually cold and intellectual, and it may take some time before he can be convinced otherwise, though you suspect that he may be right, because the King of swords is usually right about everything.

Four Card Spread

Work and business is the *seven of wands*. This shows that you are trying really hard to stay interested in your work, but you are fairly undisciplined right now except for the saving grace of the three of disks as your self card. You are taking care of only the most crucial business matters because of your intense preoccupation with your personal life. You know you are accumulating all sorts of valuable information (ace, Queen, and King of swords) that will influence your approach to your work at a later date. You need to really push yourself (Queen of swords) to feel passionate about your job or about a project that you should have finished before now (three of disks as self card). You must try not to be so distracted by your involvement with this man and by your choice about the relationship (Lovers).

Love and partnership is the *King of cups*. This signifies that the man does indeed have strong feelings and important plans for you that you are not aware of (the Sun in the difficulty-in-the-past position). His emotions run deep, even if he does not show them easily, and you have to accept that this is part of his basic personality. With the King of swords as an outcome, you can accept with great certainty that this guy hates to have his mental space invaded when he is involved with someone; he must be free to make his own decisions at his own pace. A part of him will always be unreachable to you, so forge on ahead with your own career goals. As the Queen of swords, you have much work to do (three of disks), and you are having trouble gathering the energy you need to get the job done (seven of wands in the work-and-business position). The Knight of wands as the obstacle in the Grand Cross spread also emphasizes that both of you have avoided discussing your feelings, so you have much work to do on this aspect of your personalities as well.

Trouble and conflict is *the Devil*. This shows that your biggest problems lie in the dilemma created by the worst aspects of the material world in combination with the difficulty of having to accept his King of swords/King of cups tendencies. He is putting you through some grueling tests for reasons that he keeps to himself. The things he does not say and the concerns he refuses to discuss are troubling you, and this lack of information makes you see only the dark side of his nature. He has serious doubts about this relationship, and he must clean up all his negative attitudes and habits if you two are to move forward and enjoy the bond of true love that you currently share. He may need to rid himself of a twisted image of women; otherwise he may use you to work out past discord with females in his life. Either way, he does not see the purity of the union (Sun and Lovers) the way you do. He must change his attitude toward love, or he will drag you down into the gutter of alienation.

Money and material matters is the *six of swords*. This says that even with all the emotional and practical problems you two are dealing with, your basic communication about day-to-day responsibilities is free flowing, and you make a great team. The thoughts that he is holding back from you have to do with his emotional reticence. You are kindred spirits who have mutual mental interests and compatible attitudes and values, which will help you maintain your friendship as you swim together through the murky sea of getting to know each other. Eventually you will learn the truths (Hermit) that he is keeping to himself, though this information eludes you now. His family and friends (ace of swords as outer influence) may enlighten you to the reasons behind his secretive behavior. Another interpretation of the six of swords could be that one or both of you may take a solo journey in the future to restore your mental clarity, especially if you take into account the Hermit as your hope and fear.

READING EIGHT

This Tarot reading is a direct response to the previous reading. It is meant to examine what this man is thinking about his relationship with the woman. He showed up in her cards as the two King men who keep their feelings to themselves and also as the Knight of wands who always tries to avoid commitment in love. She wanted more information on how he viewed what was happening between them and whether he envisioned a future with her.

The Grand Cross

His *self card* is the *eight of wands*. This indicates that your relationship is moving ahead much more quickly than he expected, and you have reached the doorway to a lifetime partnership sooner than he planned. He does feel a great rush of passion whenever he thinks of you and would travel across the globe to be with you. He gets carried away by a severe urgency to have you for his own, and he is desperate to create a workable alliance with you and to get beyond his emotional limitations as the King of swords/King of cups in the previous Tarot reading. This eight proves that he has the deepest desire to get past the chaos he has caused by hiding his eagerness to get your relationship off the ground, but he knows how premature his efforts may be, as you two are only in the earliest stages of intimacy. His feelings for you have taken him by surprise, and he is frightened by the intense passion he has for you. This is why the Knight of wands was your obstacle in the Grand Cross spread of the previous reading.

His *present environment* is the *nine of cups*. He feels emotionally satisfied with you. He considers his alliance with you to be future-oriented, which also was a theme in your reading. He knows his love for you will not disappear overnight, and he is struggling to become mature enough to handle true intimacy. He is completely aware of how you fit perfectly into all areas of his life, a circumstance that was emphasized by the Universe as the present environment in your Grand Cross spread. He adores you and grows to love you more each day, which is why he is itching to get things moving; but because you do not see this, you interpret his behavior as chaotic and therefore hard to understand. He is totally aware that you love him despite the coldness he projects at you as a defense mechanism (Kings of cup and sword, Knight of wands). So be secure in the knowledge that he enjoys being with you and is completely happy with you as a mate even if he gets angry or ornery because things are not moving as quickly as he had hoped.

His *obstacle* is *the Tower*. His concept of love is undergoing drastic change at this time. He never expected to meet a woman like you, and his romantic life is now beyond what he ever expected; your appearance was a total shock to him. The pattern in all his previous relationships bears no resemblance to the way he is dealing with his deep love and sexual passion for you (nine of cups and eight of wands). His belief that he would never meet such a compatible woman has fallen by the wayside, and rather quickly at that (eight of wands). He knows that his desire to wait and see what happens between you in the days to come is blocking the progress of your relationship. He is completely unsettled right now (especially in conjunction with the eight of wands), and hiding his feelings from you is definitely a calculated move on his part. Of course you are not aware of his thoughts about your relationship because of his tendency to hide the truth from you as the King of cups/King of swords personality. With the Tower as his obstacle, you can be sure it is devastating to him not to be able to show you his true feelings. You must accept that there are reasons behind his secretiveness and that he is afraid to commit himself to you. Also he may have concerns outside of your relationship that force him to wear a mask with you. It does seem as though a break-through is imminent, however, because he knows he must reveal his true self to you if the union is to survive the Tower.

His *hope and dream* is the *four of disks*. Like many people, this man holds his business dealings and his material security above all other aspects of his life. His appearance as the King of cups in your spread reiterates this truth about him. His greatest desire is to establish a practical arrangement with you, and this includes setting up a home and purchasing necessary items together. He needs to put his finances in order so he will have the resources to take care of you in a traditional manner. The five of disks in the previous reading seems to say that he does not have the money he feels he should have to be powerful and capable as a partner. He is concerned about failing you or even losing money, and his obstacle, the Tower, may symbolize a business deal that has gone bad for him recently. If his game plan has changed, he may be feeling somewhat insecure about the relationship. He is desperately seeking a new approach to deciding how the arrangement with you will work out in reality.

His *difficulty in the past* is *Strength.* This shows that up to this point in his romantic history he has not been ready for a highly evolved union of equals. He has been struggling to get himself and his life in order so he can offer you the best possible living conditions under which you can establish a powerful bond. In terms of love, any risks he has taken with you are worth it. His position of Strength says that he started straightening himself out, or at least realized he had to clean up his act, long before you came along. In the future he will need to continue to rid himself of bad habits and attitudes, and he must begin to exercise vigilance over his personality. The most constructive step he can take for himself and for the sake of the relationship is to give up anything that gets in the way of your being together.

His *last of the present* is the *Knight of wands.* This card was the obstacle in your Grand Cross reading. You can assume that in his past love life he had a tendency to run away. He has already realized that he cannot repeat this pattern, as he has an intense passion for you and he does not want to lose you. Also, repressing his desire is impossible for him; he knows this would destroy his mental and physical equilibrium (Strength). This frightened aspect of his personality is fading fast because being alienated from the one he loves just does not work for him anymore.

His *first of the future* is the *Sun.* This illustrates that he will experience an increase in consciousness about himself and will have an inspired sense of what to do in order to bring together all areas of his life. He will see the relationship in a positive light and learn how not to take you for granted. He will become more sensitive and caring and will try extra hard to bring greater joy and compatibility to your union. The Sun surfaced as your difficulty in the past in the last Tarot spread, so in the future the contentment that eludes the relationship now will grow when you two are alone, away from the pressures other people place on you.

His *future environment* is the *Page of cups.* This symbolizes his slight immaturity in the ways of love, probably because as the Knight of wands he has avoided taking the risk of deep romantic involvement. You will become aware that you have to train him to satisfy you emotionally. Despite his inexperience, he really does want to make you happy, and his intention is to support you in every way, even if his habit is to be defensive as the Kings of cup and sword and the Knight of wands. He is truly devoted to you in his heart and enjoys being by your side, and at moments when he lets down his guard you can see how he is holding on to you like a security blanket. His affection for you is evident with the nine of cups as his present environment. Any time he holds back his feelings you can be sure this is due to his fear of being hurt or rejected by you, because he retains the memory of one who broke his heart in the past. Oddly enough, he seeks sympathy from you even with the more distant aspect of his personality, which makes you feel as though he is the last one to require compassion from anyone. Also this Page can show younger people or children as an issue that will be in the forefront of his mind.

His *outer influence* is the *three of swords*. He will
have to face all of the past disappointments he has
suffered as the Page of cups. His sense of lost family
and friends is something he has to process psychologically. This card also suggests that he lives his
life for everyone but himself; he must rid himself of
this tendency if your union is to survive. He will
feel sorrow at having to leave behind certain people, places, or activities that have been a constant
part of his daily life, but his involvement with
them has alienated him from his own true self.
He will analyze whether he needs all these people in his life, and he will see that the separation
from his usual crowd must occur because these
people really do not care about him and are totally insensitive to his needs and concerns; deep
down he is really just a simple, gentle soul (Page
of cups). The hard knocks of life have forced him
to adopt the harsh King of cups/King of swords
persona as his own. His Knight of wands stance
also is a protective mechanism that he utilizes to
avoid having to face the childhood hurts that are
the source of his original pain. The Tower is making him realize that he does not need to be so defensive with you and that he can no longer run
from intimacy. The Strength trump is pushing
him to give up everyone and everything that is
not pertinent to his health and well-being, and
the three of swords is making sure he separates
himself from unhappy people in his life even if
he only removes himself from their sphere of influence psychologically. The Sun will help him to
see all of this quite clearly as he confronts his
emotional issues at last and grows into a bal-

anced adult individual who is capable of maturity.

His *hope and fear* is the *Knight of swords*. This card shows that his greatest fear is that he will unconsciously continue to act out his sword personality and hurt you because others have been cruel to him in the past. You already know from his cards that he deeply loves you and does not really want to cause you any pain, but a change in his behavioral patterns will not happen overnight. Understand that he will continue to utilize his defense of aloofness toward commitment when he feels that he is failing you or when he is drained mentally. He will tend to run whenever you try to discuss emotional issues, so it may be best to be indirect with him if you need to bring to his attention any problems you are having with the relationship.

His *outcome* is the *King of cups*. This card can signal that, as happy as you may be in the future, his secretive nature is something you must come to accept. Perhaps he refuses to express his feelings so as to avoid injury, or maybe he simply does not want you to know his plans for you or his business dealings. His intention is not to hurt you (Page of cups), but his life experiences have conditioned him to retreat emotionally by utilizing anger and withdrawing his energy from a woman in order to cover up his great fear of intimacy (Knight of wands). He needs to conquer this tendency with all the support of the Sun and Strength trumps. He will always retain an aura of mystery for you, and though he adores you, his nature is not to share or discuss his feelings. He will be a tough nut to crack, and you will have to expend much energy (seven of wands in your reading) to figure out what is going on in his heart and mind in the days to come.

Four Card Spread

Work and business is the *six of cups*. This shows him doing his best to become a loving and lovable person. He wants to grow with you and learn to give of himself emotionally and express his feelings openly to you. You need to be aware of his depth of happiness in finding you (nine of cups) and try not to become distracted from this truth by his personality disorder. He also should try to establish a work routine that he enjoys immensely, and the renewal factor of the six of cups suggests that he would be in better shape if he had a new project or a new job to challenge him professionally. His being excited by his work would directly affect how your relationship proceeds, even if it takes him a while to figure out what he wants to do next—though with the eight of wands as his self card, he is dying to get involved in something new.

Love and partnership is *the Juggler*. This card depicts more complexities in his behavior. He will be tricky and deceptive in dealing with you. This trump reiterates his tendency not to be verbal about his plans and shows how he really does mistrust women due to bad experiences with them in the past (Page of cups). He is doing all he can behind the scenes to move your relationship forward, and he has big plans for you that he is doing his best to hide. He is totally aware of the seriousness of your connection and is utilizing all his willpower to move the union forward and create a life you can ultimately share and enjoy; it seems as though his urgency (eight of wands) is greater than the reality he can bring about at this time. On a higher level, the position of this trump shows his magical attraction and intense interest in you without question, especially with the influence of the King of cups as his outcome.

Trouble and conflict is *Juno*. The consort of the Juggler with her Priestess self is equal to this man's Juggler energy. It has already been established that he is approaching the relationship with all the illusory qualities associated with the Juggler, but your Juno nature is unsettling to him. Perhaps he is uncomfortable with a woman who seems to know him intuitively to the depths of his soul, or maybe he has never been with one who is totally in touch with her spiritual side. He feels spooked by the fact that you two share an unspoken bond and have similar views on life. Though his ego is putting up walls of confusion between you, he knows in his heart that you are his woman, and he cannot ignore the cosmic connection between you two.

Money and material matters is the *five of disks*. This card is also your first of the future. The placement of the five of disks in his money position suggests that he does not have the necessary funds to actualize his plans for you. If he obviously does have the material wherewithal to make his dreams a reality, however, the interpretation of this disk becomes more complex. It is likely that he is hiding his wealth, which may be one of the reasons behind his reserve. He may own more than meets the eye, and he may keep this to himself to protect his assets.

The appearance of being poor or his tendency to be overly cheap may be a ruse, or perhaps he grew up impoverished and always had to worry about money. Either way, he has trouble shaking the fear that he could suddenly lose everything. You should be aware that this may be one of his psychological problems. On another note, he may want to simplify his life-style and let go of many of the material commitments to others that prevent him from living the way he wants to (three of swords). Nonetheless, this attitude of his toward money will hit you square in the face in the days ahead due to the position of the five of disks in your Grand Cross spread.

WHY HAS THE TRUTH BEEN COVERED UP FOR 40 YEARS?

__THE ROSWELL INCIDENT
The Classic Study of UFO Contact
by Charles Berlitz and William L. Moore
0-425-12602-1/$3.95

As the most important UFO encounter of our century, the facts about the incident are still being hidden from the American public. This ground-breaking book not only explores every aspect of the mysterious UFO crash near Roswell, New Mexico, but also probes the bizarre government cover-up that began within hours of the discovery and has continued right up to the present day.

UFO'S <u>DO</u> EXIST...

__THE UFO ABDUCTORS
by Brad Steiger 0-425-11165-2/$3.50

Brad Steiger, the world renowned authority on unexplained phenomena, presents a vast collection of documented UFO encounters and abductions. His provocative theories proved answers to the most puzzling questions: Why are they here? What do they want? And how will they change the fate of the human race?
